# LINSEED PAINT AND OIL

## A PRACTICAL GUIDE TO TRADITIONAL PRODUCTION AND APPLICATION

*Michiel Brouns*

THE CROWOOD PRESS

## Dedication

*Veur Pap*

'... the world is not given by his fathers, but borrowed from his children.'
Wendell Berry, *Unforeseen Wilderness: Kentucky's Red River Gorge*

'Take proper care of your monuments, and you will not need to restore them.'
John Ruskin, *The Seven Lamps of Architecture*

First published in 2023 by
The Crowood Press Ltd
Ramsbury, Marlborough
Wiltshire SN8 2HR

enquiries@crowood.com

**www.crowood.com**

**British Library Cataloguing-in-Publication Data**
A catalogue record for this book is available from the British Library.

ISBN 978 0 7198 4225 2

**Acknowledgements**
The Brouns & Co. Team
Katie Anderson-Morrison
Ian Stokes
Shona Munro
Arja Källbom
Ruth Miller
Peter Galloway
Everett Schram
Dr Benjamin Stern
Dr Richard Telford CChem CSci FRSC
Belinda Whitehead

Typeset by Simon and Sons
Cover design by Blue Sunflower Creative
Printed and bound in India by Parksons Graphics

## Contents

The value of old buildings is indisputable. Thompson M. Mayes' *Why Old Places Matter*[1] is an excellent work on this. It highlights the worth of historic buildings not only in terms of their economic and environmental terms, but also in the way that they contribute to our sense of continuity, identity and belonging. Whichever way you choose to look at it, old buildings matter and we need to ensure that we do everything we can to keep them habitable and usable. Linseed paint fulfils a much bigger role in this than is generally understood.

Of course, caring for old buildings can consume our time and our money. For many people, so-called 'historic buildings' are synonymous with the idea of cold, damp money pits. It's difficult to come up with a definition for historic buildings without evoking images of listed buildings and the associated complex regulations. In the context of using linseed paint and other traditional building materials and techniques, I find it most useful to describe properties as 'historic' or 'modern' on the basis of whether they're built using solid wall constructions or wall cavities. This difference is really what determines the requirement of the building in terms of breathability, water absorption and retention. Obviously, there is a time and a place for modern building materials, but very few are compatible with historic solid wall structures. Personally, I do not believe there is any necessity for plastic or chemical materials in these structures, as arguably they do more damage than good.

In recent decades, the UK has experienced something of a boom in the understanding of traditional building materials and how to care for old buildings. A great deal of knowledge has made its way over from Scandinavia, the Netherlands, France and Germany, where many of these skills, products and techniques are very much still in common use. (Though, of course, even in these countries, traditional fabrics and materials have been relegated to the periphery since World War II, when the general industry focus switched to plastics and quick fixes.)

And yet, despite this growing understanding, linseed paint still remains in the dominion of specialist knowledge. Browse any bookshop or architectural library stocking DIY and restoration titles and you will find a wide selection of titles dedicated to lime paint, lime wash and lime tender, but I am yet to find a single publication on linseed paint. Even Coen Eggen's seminal work *Vakwerkbouw*[2], about Tudor-style wattle and daub constructions, only dedicated one paragraph to linseed paint, though almost every piece of timber in the buildings discussed would have been treated in linseed oil, stand oil or linseed paint.

It's true that linseed paint has a very specific application, but it was also far more widely used than its little-known reputation might suggest. It is historically accurate, completely environmentally friendly and – perhaps most importantly – incredibly effective. The aim of this book is to share knowledge about linseed paint, its history and its correct application. I am grateful for the opportunity to add my little bit of expertise to the ever-growing world of building restoration and preservation.

## What is Linseed Paint?

Linseed paint is a type of paint that has been used for many thousands of years. It is made by combining linseed oil with a range of natural raw earth pigments.

Unlike the ingredients typically found in modern paints, linseed oil is made using naturally occurring ingredients. It's made by pressing the dried, ripened seeds of flax plants (*Linum usitatissimum*), which belong to the Linaceae plant family. This family also includes plants used to produce linen, though flax plants grown for fibre tend to be tall, early maturing plants, while those grown for seeds are usually shorter and need longer to mature fully.

Flax plants produce flax fruits, or 'bolls', that are made up of five cells. When these have fully matured, they will contain ten seeds. The seeds can be warm-pressed or cold-pressed. Warm-pressing seeds gives a higher yield, but cold-pressing is usually a better option, as it results in fewer impurities.

The oil that results from this process is extremely versatile and has a huge number of applications, from DIY to health food supplementation. It even plays a role in the making of linoleum flooring. Linseed oil is classed as a drying oil due to its high content of di- and tri-unsaturated esters. This makes it even more versatile, as it means that it can be effectively combined with other oils to create an even wider range of derivatives.

According to historical records, flaxseed was first used around 8000/9000BC in Turkey, Iran, Jordan and Syria. Nowadays, it is grown in more than fifty countries. The biggest producer is Canada, followed by China, the USA and India.[3]

## Linseed Paint and Me

I grew up in South Limburg, which is the southernmost part of the Netherlands, wedged in-between Germany and Wallonia, the French-speaking part of Belgium. Because of this, I was brought up surrounded by an eclectic mix of architecture, where Modernist buildings happily sit beside – or even within – thirteenth- and fourteenth-century churches. To see this in action, I'd recommend a visit to Maastricht to see the Kruisherenklooster, a gothic, fifteenth-century monastery that now houses a luxury hotel, and the Dominicanenkerk, a thirteenth-century church turned destination bookshop.

However, the most typical historical buildings found in South Limburg are the *vakwerk* farms and houses. These are typical timber-frame, wattle and daub Tudor-style constructions – just like the ones explored in Coen Eggen's book *Vakwerkbouw*.[4] Though Limburg has been firmly part of the Netherlands since 1830, this was not always the case. Geologically, culturally and even linguistically, it forms part of the Euregio region, which spreads across the Netherlands, Belgium and Germany. The *vakwerk* cottages are a part of this region and are an offshoot of the far more ornate *Fachwerk* houses found all over Germany. This type of wattle and daub construction is also found in relatively large numbers in the UK, mainly in southern England.

My father's grandparents bought a *vakwerk* cottage in the hamlet of Termaar in 1921 and it stayed in the family for two generations. As a child, I lived close to it, passing it each day on my journey to school. As such, this type of architecture became part of my DNA and is one reason why I developed such a great interest in

Field of flax.

history and architecture and the various ways in which they intersect.

One of my first jobs was in the sales department of a ceramic tile manufacturer in Maastricht. I used to take the bus to work, which meant I had a fifteen-minute changeover in the town of Gulpen. While killing time on the high street, I decided to go into a shop called Kwarts & Co. for a look. Inside, I was awestruck by everything on offer, including ironmongery, encaustic tiles, lime plaster, timber flooring and linseed paint, and right there and then I asked the owner, Haske Van Zadelhoff, if he was looking for any employees. As it happened, he was. I started there a few weeks later and it very much changed the course of my life. It was as far removed as possible from the corporate world I had started out in. Haske taught me almost everything there was to know about the use of traditional building materials and techniques, including the use of colour and pigmentation and the practice of resolving damp issues in historical buildings. I learned far more in the three years I worked there than I could ever have done in any other setting.

Shortly after moving to the UK in January 2006, I decided to set up Histoglass, a company specialising in insulation glazing designed to be installed in existing historical windows. This really thin double glazing was a product that Haske used to sell at Kwarts & Co. and I anticipated that it would be of interest to people in the UK. To begin with, I targeted architectural practices, giving presentations to thousands of architects all over the UK and, within five years, Histoglass Ltd was the leading supplier of thin double glazing for high-end residential and commercial properties.

One of the main questions I'd be asked at the end of these presentations would be something along the lines of: 'When we're restoring windows to put in these glazing systems, which paint would you recommend?' I'd assumed that every architect (particularly restoration architects) would know about linseed paint, but whenever I suggested it, I was usually met with blank looks. When I realised that such a valuable, historically correct paint wasn't widely known, I knew I had to do something about it.

When Brouns & Co. first launched in 2011 (initially under the name Histocolour and then Oricalcum), the first stock order fitted on to a single IKEA Billy bookcase. I set out with the hope that the business would be a dynamic thing that would evolve over time. This has certainly been the case and the whole operation, along with the stock levels, has grown considerably over time.

Histoglass Brouns & Co. glazing and paint has been used in locations including the Tower of London, the Queen's House National Maritime Museum, various colleges at the universities of

Michiel in front of the family *vakwerk*.

Cambridge and Oxford, the Old War Offices, Chatsworth House, Woburn Abbey, Windsor Castle, Mount Vernon, the Olson House and various other stately homes and royal palaces. I have also worked with organisations including the National Trust, English Heritage, Historic England, Historic Environment Scotland, the Landmark Trust and Historic New England, as well as the American College of Building Arts and National Park Services. This includes work with architects all over the world, particularly in the UK and USA, as the building vernacular is very similar. The extensive use of timber in US historical buildings means that, traditionally, many of these would have been treated with linseed oil or linseed paint, which means that my knowledge tends to translate perfectly.

Over the years, I've had the pleasure of learning even more about linseed paint from experts including Gunnar Ottosson from the Swedish company Ottosson Färgmakeri and Thor Grabow from the Danish company Linolie & Pigment. Arja Källbom has also been incredibly generous and forthcoming with answering many questions for me over the years. I have also done a lot of my own research, including working with Bradford University to use high-field NMR spectroscopy to study samples of our paints and oils at a macromolecular level. There are some excellent historical works on paint, pigments and renovation, and I have aimed to collect as much of this research material as I can, in the original language wherever possible. This ensures that I am not relying on the thought pattern and approach of one particular locale.

For me, learning about linseed oil and linseed paint is an ongoing quest. I now know infinitely more than I did a decade ago and no doubt will learn a great deal more in the next one. Though you can rest assured that you will find everything you need to know about the benefits and use of linseed oil and paint in this book, I, like everyone else, always have more to learn.

## Chapter One

# The History of Linseed Paint

Linseed oil is often said to be as old as the hills. Though it probably isn't *quite* that old, there is certainly enough evidence to link it back to multiple ancient civilisations, including Ancient Egypt.

In 2013, the UK's Channel 4 aired a documentary about the remains of Tutankhamun called *Tutankhamun: The Mystery of the Burnt Mummy*. In particular, the documentary set out to address the question of why the king's remains are so badly charred, and why this appears to have happened while the mummy was sealed inside the coffin.[5] After much careful analysis, the experts determined that the reason for the charring was because the mummification of Tutankhamun's remains had to happen quickly – most likely because of war or civil unrest – and those who carried out the process were therefore careless. The experts' theory was that rags soaked with linseed oil, which had been used in the process, were left on the mummy and caught fire, causing the remains to burn inside the sarcophagus.

Not all scholars agree on this and Professor Ben Sherman from the University of Bradford had his doubts when I discussed it with him. Though it's certainly an interesting theory, whether or not linseed oil was used on that particular occasion as part of the process is more or less irrelevant. What does matter, and what is known without any doubt, is that the use of linseed oil and paint can be traced back for thousands of years.

## How is Linseed Paint Made?

Historically, linseed paint was mixed in individual quantities by hand. In the 1723 book, *The Art of Painting in Oyl*, John Smith wrote:

Lay ... two Spoonfuls of the colour on the midst of your Stone, and put a little Linseed Oyl to it, ... then with your Muller mix it together ... 'till it come to the Consistence of an Oyntment ... and smooth as the most curious Sort of Butter.[6]

In essence, modern linseed paint production has not changed a great deal from these instructions. Though, of course, when making linseed paint in industrial quantities, a muller and stone is obviously not an efficient way of doing things. On an industrial scale, the muller and stone are replaced with a triple roller mill. Though significantly larger and more sophisticated, a triple roller mill still achieves the main purpose in exactly the same way – by grinding pigment into boiled linseed oil to form a paste.

Quicker production methods do exist, such as using high-speed machinery to stir oil and pigments together to disperse the pigment. However, this does not result in the same smooth, fine texture as is achieved by the grinding process. Another method involves what is essentially a big column drill with an extended head that uses ball bearings to grind pigment into oil, but this method would only be able to create the correct consistency with days and days of work. If that wasn't reason enough for this method to be considered unworkable, the pressure released by the drill would heat the oil and pigments to such an extent that they would need to be left to cool every couple of hours. Arguably, this is one of those instances where the original method just can't be beaten, though obviously it's been refined over the centuries as new technology and equipment has come along.

Once the initial paste of pigment and boiled linseed oil has been created, additional pigment pastes can be mixed in to achieve the correct hue. Finally, more boiled oil is added in order to reach the desired consistency. Real linseed paint should only contain a mix of natural pigments without any synthetic colourants, as these are not stable enough in boiled linseed oil. Modern linseed oil generally also contains a small proportion of natural solvents (such as balsam turpentine) and drying agents.

## The Early History of Linseed Oil

### Early history in Europe

It all began with the flax plant, officially known as *Linum usitatissimum*. This multipurpose plant is not only responsible for linseed oil, which is derived from the seeds, but also linen, which is made from the plant fibres.

Growing and cultivating flax plants is an ancient activity, as is the making of linen. Evidence of linen-making has been found by archaeologists in Neolithic settlements in the Jura Mountains of Switzerland.[7] With the knowledge we have now about the ancient use of linseed oil, we can safely assume that wherever there was linen production, there was also linseed oil. Over the centuries, the growing and processing of flax became a commercially minded operation. By the Middle Ages it was big business, especially in the lower Rhine region of Germany. At the time, Germany made and exported more linen than anywhere else in the world.[8]

This is also the point at which linseed oil became widely used as a building product. Evidence of this can be seen at the Museum of Cultural History in Lund, Sweden, which collects old buildings from all over the country and reconstructs them together in one place for people to visit. Amongst these buildings are cabins from the 1300s, which still include some of the original timbers. There is evidence to suggest that these timbers have only ever been treated with pine tar and linseed oil.

We know from the paintings of Vermeer and Rembrandt that the use of linseed paint was very common in the art world by the 1600s. However, by this point it was also being widely used in building applications outside Scandinavia, certainly in Amsterdam, Delft and Leiden. By the late 1600s and early 1700s, this had spread even further and linseed paint was being used extensively in England. It was at this time that John Smith published the first known account of how to make and apply linseed oil. My copy of his book *The Art of Painting in Oyl* is a fifth edition and was published in 1723 (the first edition was published in 1676). Smith wrote:

> The whole Treatise being to full Compleat, and to exactly fitted to the meanest Capacity, that all Persons whatsoever, may be able by these Directions, to Paint in Oyl Colours all manner of Timber work; that require either Use, Beauty of Preservation, from the violence or Injury of the Weather.[9]

Though Germany dominated the flax trade early on, by the sixteenth century there was a wide corridor of flax production stretching from western Switzerland to the Rhine, up to Denmark and Sweden.[10] The huge trade in flax, linen and linseed oil would have meant that the people who lived in these areas were hugely familiar with linseed oil and its uses.

*The Art of Painting in Oyl.*

It's only natural, then, that when European nations began expanding into the 'new world' of the Americas, the people that travelled there took their knowledge of linseed oil with them.

## Reaching the New World

By the late 1500s, Sweden, the Netherlands (Holland), France and Spain were battling for dominance, both in terms of religion and land. This quest eventually led them to expand into the 'New World' of the Americas. Spain began to dominate the largest part of South and middle America, but Sweden and the Netherlands were more interested in parts of North America, as was France. France was on the rise as a world power and had its sights firmly fixed on what is now the Hudson Bay area, along with most of eastern Canada. The

most effective way for cultures, habits, languages and architecture to spread is by the movement of people. As European settlements expanded into other parts of the world, they took all these things with them.

The later 1500s and early 1600s were a fairly turbulent period in terms of religion, with convictions and affiliations frequently changing, especially in England. A group of persecuted Protestants fled Yorkshire, Nottinghamshire and Derbyshire to seek religious sanctuary in Leiden, in the Netherlands. This religious persecution fuelled the expansion of Protestant Northern European nations into the New World, and the Leiden Protestants set sail in 1620, first on the *Speedwell* from Delfshaven, in the Netherlands, then onwards on the *Mayflower* from England.

The *Mayflower* is best known for the Pilgrims, but at least half of the passengers on board were classified as 'strangers'. These strangers were non-Puritans

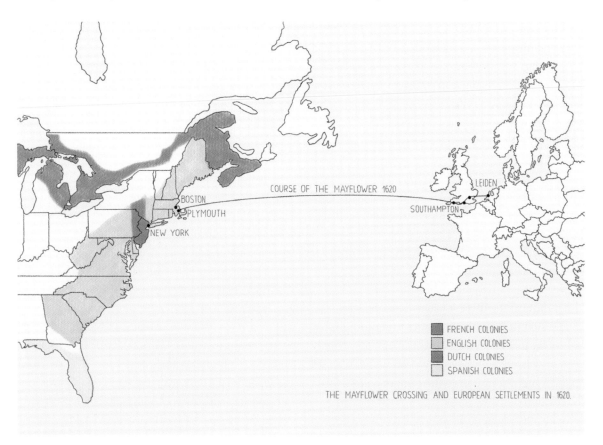

THE MAYFLOWER CROSSING AND EUROPEAN SETTLEMENTS IN 1620.

FRENCH COLONIES
ENGLISH COLONIES
DUTCH COLONIES
SPANISH COLONIES

Map depicting the journey of the *Mayflower* and first European settlement areas.

simply hoping to start a better life in what they thought would be Virginia.[11] Many of these individuals had been selected on the basis of their usefulness and physical fitness. This meant that they were disproportionately young men, most barely out of their teens, who were skilled in rough trades such as carpentry, thatching and general building work. Many of these strangers would therefore have been well-practised in using linseed oil and its derivatives for building applications. Indeed, on their initial voyages they took some essential tools and building materials with them, including linseed oil and pigments.

When the settlers reached America and established the Plymouth Colony, linseed oil was one of the building products they used to do this. Not only would it likely have been used for timber preservation, but Patricia and Scott Deetz also note in their book *The Times of their Lives: Life, Love and Death in Plymouth Colony*: 'the house's tiny, barely translucent windows were made of linseed-coated parchment.'[12]

It was not only persecuted Protestants from Europe who took linseed oil with them to the Americas. By the late seventeenth century, northern Ireland had emerged as a leader in the flax trade. This would have cemented local knowledge about linseed oil and its uses just in time for the first wave of Irish immigration to America in the early eighteenth century. Indeed, the Northern Irish helped to bring the flax plant to the New World, just as nearly every other group of European emigrants did.[13]

## The Industrial Revolution

The Industrial Revolution had a huge impact on the production of linseed oil, just as it did on almost everything else. Though flax plants had already been processed in a reasonably commercial manner for many centuries before this, the scale increased rapidly.

By the late eighteenth century, there were dozens of linseed oil processing plants in the north of England alone, particularly in Lancashire, Manchester, the Midlands and Yorkshire. Ditherington Flax Mill, one of the most famous, was built in Shrewsbury in 1797. Interestingly, it was the world's first iron-framed building and is therefore considered a precursor of the modern skyscraper. Because of this, many believe the mill to be one of the most important buildings of the modern age.[14]

Linseed oil production also increased massively in America during this period. Census records from 1810 show that there were more than seventy mills between Berks County, Montgomery County and York County in Pennsylvania (all regions with large Germanic populations). Much of the oil produced in these mills was sold to paint manufacturers in Philadelphia.[15]

## The Modernist Movement

For centuries, linseed paint was used on everything from windows and doors to cladding, boats and bridges. Then we come to the outbreak of World War II. This was a watershed moment in the building trade, not just because of the sheer scale of the rebuilding that was needed across Europe afterwards, but also because of the significant mental shift that took place in architecture.

The Modernist Movement that had begun in the 1920s and 1930s took flight, meaning that the 'old' established forms of architecture suddenly seemed less appealing than the use of concrete, large expanses of glazing and plastics. You may remember the moment in the 1967 film *The Graduate* where Mr McGuire (played by Walter Brook) says to Benjamin Braddock (played by Dustin Hoffman): 'Plastics … there's a great future in plastics.' He wasn't wrong.

In the period after World War II, there was an enormous mountain of refinery 'waste' left over from the war effort. This consisted of mainly acrylics and latexes, which are waste products made when refining crude oil into fuels. Over time, scientists discovered how this oil could be synthesised on a vast scale and modern 'plastic' paint was born.

Example of rotting timber due to modern paints trapping moisture, Newport, RI.

Looking back, we can see that many of these plastics did not quite deliver on their promise. From the 1980s onwards, a lot of these new plastic building materials, particularly modern paints, that had been introduced to old buildings began to fail. Mostly, this resulted in a lot of problems with damp and an awful lot of rotten timber. Perhaps this is in no small part why we now find ourselves caught in a culture of short-term fixes.

## Is Linseed Paint Still Relevant Today?

There's no doubt that linseed oil and paint have a phenomenal track record, but you might find yourself wondering if a product that was first used over 3,000 years ago is really still the right choice today. It's a valid question, but one on which the facts really do speak for themselves.

After all, not only does linseed paint provide unparalleled rot-protection for timber, it's also incredibly durable. A well-painted surface will last for ten or fifteen years, and even then it will probably just need treating with a coat of raw linseed oil to freshen it up. This makes it an excellent investment, especially when you consider the fact that linseed oil is very affordable in the first place. Per cost of square metre painted, exterior linseed paint is highly competitive with other perceived high-quality petrochemical paint brands.

There is another reason why linseed paint is particularly relevant to us in the twenty-first century: its impressive environmental credentials. There are only trace elements of volatile organic compounds (VOCs) in linseed paint, no plastics and no unpronounceable ingredients: just linseed oil and natural pigments. This makes it the perfect cradle to cradle product, with little to no environmental impact. The building and architectural industries are not necessarily making as big a drive towards environmental sustainability as they perhaps should be, but choosing natural products like linseed paint is a great place to start.

## Chapter Two

# Different Uses of Linseed Oil

The seeds of the flax plant are harvested and processed into oil in a variety of forms, known by a range of different names. Some of these types of oil are mixed with pigment to make linseed paint, while others are used neat, or mixed with various substances to make other forms of building materials.

Though there are key differences among these various types of linseed oil, they all share the same chemical make-up. Linseed oil is based on linolenic acid and contains a high number of double bonds. These bonds are broken as part of a polymerisation process, which is set in motion by exposure to oxygen. This creates chemical cross links, which, in turn, form a weather-resistant film called linoxin.

In this chapter you will find a guide to the different forms of linseed oil available and which one might be the most suitable for your project.

## PURE LINSEED OILS

### Flaxseed or flax oil

Linseed oil that is pure enough to be edible is generally known as flaxseed or flax oil. This is often sold in health food shops and is intended for food supplementation. However, I would suggest checking the packaging of any flaxseed or flax oil very carefully before adding it to food, as many types have added ingredients that are not intended for consumption.

Flax seed.

### Raw linseed oil

Raw linseed oil is unprocessed oil, without any added driers or thinners. Much of the low-cost linseed oil on the market falls into this category. These cheaper products are often made from warm-pressed oils, which tend to contain a lot of impurities and proteins.

Raw linseed oil is generally not very effective when used in linseed paint, or on its own as a wood treatment. This is because the impurities and proteins result in a high risk of mould and algae growth. Even if you choose to use a purer, cold-pressed raw linseed oil, you will need to use very thin coats, as it does not dry particularly well.

For those who are interested in the chemistry behind linseed oil, raw linseed oil mainly consists of linoleic and oleic acid with three-quarters polyunsaturated fatty acids and very high Omega 3 and 6

Raw linseed oil.

Boiled linseed oil.

content. High-grade raw linseed oil is often used as an additive in animal feed.

## Boiled linseed oil

Boiled linseed oil is created when raw linseed oil is boiled for hours at a particular temperature. This changes the viscosity, chemical structure and polymerisation of the oil, resulting in a thicker, altered carbon bond that dries more quickly. In some cases, a small quantity of natural drying agents such as cobalt, manganese or calcium are added as part of the process. Boiled oil is deeper and richer in colour than raw linseed oil. It can be used effectively to treat furniture and indoor woodwork. It is also the main ingredient in exterior linseed paint.

## Double-boiled linseed oil, or 'Hollandic boiling method'

There are some products on the market that claim to be 'double-boiled' or boiled using the Hollandic method. This is generally marketing-spiel rather than a genuine

description. This method would involve adding litharge or lead at 280°C, which isn't currently possible. Besides, there is no benefit to boiling linseed oil twice.

## Stand oil or polymerised linseed oil

Stand oil is a specialised form of boiled linseed oil. It is made by heating raw linseed oil at close to 300°C in a vacuum for a few days. This creates a very thick oil that has more of an elastic coating than standard boiled linseed oil.

This form of linseed oil is most commonly used by artists as part of certain paint techniques. It is not usually used in architectural paintwork, as the thickness of stand oil is difficult to work with over a large surface area.

## Sun-thickened, or sun-bleached linseed oil

Raw linseed oil can be thickened by setting it in large trays and exposing it to sunlight for a few months. This increases the elasticity of the oil and reduces yellowing.

## Flammability

Linseed oil and paint are not flammable in their own right in the course of normal use. However, it is possible for rags that have been soaked in linseed oil (or have been used to wipe a brush or clean up spilt paint) to combust spontaneously. Avoid this by making sure to soak any rags used with linseed oil or paint thoroughly under the tap before throwing them away. Alternatively, you can leave used rags out in the sun to dry out completely before disposing of them.

Bucket of water with rags.

Sun-thickened oil is not generally used on its own, but it can be a useful additive in linseed paint, especially when it is particularly important to create an even finish. Like stand oil, sun-thickened linseed oil is generally more relevant to artists than to people refinishing window frames.

## COMBINED LINSEED OILS

### Danish oil

Danish oil is usually made by blending boiled linseed oil or stand oil with tung oil (which is made by pressing the seeds of the tung tree). The combination of these oils is often used either as a wood primer, or to create a hard-wearing satin finish. Unfortunately, there is no standard recipe for Danish oil, which means that products bearing this name can vary wildly in grade and quality.

### Linseed putty

Linseed putty is made by mixing boiled linseed oil with chalk. Though you will find a range of versions on the market, true linseed putty should not contain any solvents or plastics. The colour of the natural putty should be an off-white (often described as 'antique white'). This is caused by the linseed oil having a yellowing effect on the bright white of the chalk.

Linseed putty is a versatile material that can be used for glazing as well as small wood repairs. (I would suggest a maximum repair area of $2.5 \times 2.5$cm [$1 \times 1$in], as anything bigger will require another filler to be used in conjunction with the linseed putty.) For best results, knead the putty before use to make sure that it's really pliable. Linseed putty keeps for a long time, unless it dries out. When storing linseed putty, I recommend pouring some linseed oil into the top of the tub, as this will make it keep much longer.

Linseed putty.

Pouring some raw linseed oil on top of the linseed putty will prevent it from drying out.

Make sure the whole surface is covered.

A final note on usage: linseed putty can be overpainted with linseed paint as soon as the putty has a skin that's thick enough not to show brush marks. The putty and the paint will then bond and cure together to give a strong, durable finish. Simply rub the paint with some raw linseed oil for nourishment whenever required. Acrylic paint does not adhere properly to linseed putty, so overpainting with this is likely to result in moisture getting trapped in the timber, the paint flaking and the putty becoming brittle.

## TAR OIL

Tar oil is made by combining raw linseed oil with pine tar. This can be considered to be the mother of all wood treatments, with evidence of its use dating all the way back to Mesolithic times.

Pine tar is formed when pine is carbonised at very high temperatures. Traditionally, only pine stumps and roots are used to make pine tar. The following passage, from Claessons Trätjära's look at historical tar wood production in Sweden, explains how the tar is made:

After the resinous pine stubs have been pulled up the wood is cut, divided and dried before the burning takes place. The tar pile is usually built up as a cone of fir that is covered, first with birch-bark then with clay soil, in order to give a tight surface. At the bottom of this a 'shoe' is placed to collect the tar before the plug is pulled and the tar runs through a channel into the collection barrel. The next stage is to put the wood in a given pattern in the pile .... When the wood has formed a pile of the right size, it is covered with easily burnt wood [kindle] which will enable an easy start to the burning process. The pile is then covered with peat, moss or earth in order to be properly airtight.

The burning is started by lighting the wood around the base of the pile through holes in the pile covering. The fire should spread itself

Using tar oil.

over the outer layer from the bottom up and then slowly burn through the pile inwards and downwards.

It is first when the firing has reached the centre of the pile that the tar starts showing itself, first in the form of tar water, which is soon replaced by the best, pure, light tar. Towards the end the tar becomes more viscous and pitch like. In the trial project, the tar started running out after about 24 hours of lighting the fire.[16]

Initially, pine tar was used as an adhesive in weapon production, then later as a lubricant for Roman chariots and later still for medicinal and veterinary uses.[17] When mixed with linseed oil, pine tar becomes the perfect wood preservation product and has incredible, long-lasting benefits.

One of the best places to see tar oil in action is in the Norwegian medieval stave churches, of which there are twenty-eight still standing. The oldest, Urnes, dates to the 1130s, though some of the timber that was used to build it, including two foundation beams and almost all of the wall planks, actually came from an earlier church, built in the 1070s. These stave churches were built entirely from locally available pine, without the use of any nails. All of the timber was treated with tar oil, which over the years turned the buildings dark brown or even black. Tar oil is still used to maintain these medieval churches today, a practice that is explored in Inger Marie Egenberg's fascinating dissertation on the subject.[18] According to Egenberg, Dalbränd pine tar is the preferred pine tar for this application, which is made primarily from resin-containing heartwood from old stumps.

The Nordic Tar Network is doing an excellent job of keeping the traditional production and application methods alive. Its annual conference brings together every expert in this field.

In the UK, the traditional lychgate in Whixley, North Yorkshire, is a great example of a situation where timber really benefits from a nourishing coat of tar oil.

For the last few centuries, Sweden, Finland and Russia have been the main producers of pine tar. However, North America was also a fairly big production centre, especially at the beginning of the eighteenth century when Britain encouraged its North American colonies to replace their Scandinavian pine tar supply, which had been interrupted by Russia invading Sweden and Finland.[19] Even when Britain switched back to Scandinavian pine tar, tar oil remained the dominant timber treatment in Virginia and Maryland well into the second half of the eighteenth century.[20]

## How to apply tar oil

The process of applying tar oil is really straightforward. It is best to apply it in summer, as the higher the temperature, the thinner the tar oil will be. If you do need to apply tar oil in cool weather, you may need to warm it before you begin. The best way to do this is *au bain-marie*, that is, by placing the tin in a container that is sitting in warm water.

For best results when applying tar oil, use the following steps:

1. Make sure that the surface is completely clear and free from dust and algae. This can be achieved either by brushing the surface with a good hand brush, or by washing it with linseed soap or brown soap.
2. Make any necessary repairs to the wood, ideally using oakum to fill any gaps or cracks.
3. Give the tar oil a really good stir.
4. Apply the tar oil liberally to the surface.

It is important to take precautions while using tar oil. This includes wearing protective clothing and soaking any of the rags you have used in water before throwing them away.

Lychgate – before.

Before being treated with tar oil.

Stirring the tar oil.

Scrubbing the surface ready for the tar oil.

Pouring the tar oil.

Make sure to apply the tar oil really deep by brush.

Really work the product into the grain.

Lychgate – halfway.

Applying the tar oil by brush.

Tar oil being applied.

Finished.

## Oakum

Oakum is a traditional filler material made from old, untwisted rope drenched in tar oil. It can be used to create watertight seals, which is why its traditional use was in the marine world. However, it's also extremely useful for sealing log cabins (put a layer between logs or beams) and for filling gaps between walls and window frames.

If you're using oakum to fill a window gap, make sure that you pack the oakum in tightly by using a making iron, then finish with lime putty or lime caulking. Both of these options will keep moisture out without trapping any moisture that does get in. I have seen many Georgian and Victorian sash cases that were installed this way a few hundred years ago and yet still look like they were only recently installed.

### The downsides of tar oil

Of course, there are some downsides to tar oil. Though it is an excellent timber treatment, it is not as long-lasting as some other options. Historically, such as in the case of the Norwegian stave churches, it is thought that it only needed to be reapplied every three years. However, modern tar oil often needs reapplying as frequently as once a year, especially on areas that are very exposed to the weather.[21]

As is often the case, 'natural' does not necessarily mean that something is healthy for humans or animals. Wood tars do contain a certain amount of potentially harmful components, albeit in very small quantities. Because of this, it's advisable to wear protective clothing when using wood tar or tar oil, especially if you do so on a regular basis.

Oakum.

## Chapter Three

# Why Does Linseed Paint Work So Well?

Nowadays, the main considerations for choosing one particular type of paint over another seem to be aesthetics and marketing. Though there's no doubt that paint and the various hues it comes in can be beautiful to look at – and significantly influence our state of mind – this cannot be the whole story. Rather, we should be giving due consideration to what paint is made of, what its embodied energy is and what its function is.

Linseed paint is a great example of this. Not only does this natural, historical paint have a wonderful decorative effect, it's also very hard-working. Its main role is to protect from the elements: it can stop timber from rotting and prevent metal from rusting. Essentially, it works by forming a sacrificial coat over whatever surface it's painted on in order to protect it.

Broadly speaking, there are two types of historical paint: those that are made by dispersing pigments in water and those that are made by dispersing pigments in oil. We often hear the terms 'water-based' and 'oil-based' in relation to modern acrylic paints, which can be thinned either with water or with oils

## Modern 'oil' and acrylic paints

Modern oil paints are typically known as 'alkyd' paints. Instead of pigment being suspended in linseed oil, alkyd paints are typically formed by dissolving an alkyd resin in a thinner. Most commercially available 'oil-based' paints are a mix of pigments and a solution containing alkyd resin and petroleum-based solvents such as naptha.

The conventional wall paints used today, often known as 'emulsion', are acrylic paints. These are made by suspending pigments in acrylic polymer emulsion. Other ingredients, such as plasticisers, silicone oils, defoamers, stabilisers and metal soaps are often added. In the USA, this type of paint is often known as 'latex paint'.

such as white spirit or turps. However, this is a bit confusing as the only real oil- and water-based paints are natural paints, not petrochemical derivatives.

## Types of natural paint

| Natural water-based paints | Natural oil-based paints |
|---|---|
| <ul><li>lime washes</li><li>clay paints</li><li>distempers</li></ul> | <ul><li>linseed paint</li></ul> |
| These paints were traditionally – and still should be – applied to plaster and stone. | Traditionally, oil-based paints were mostly applied to timber, metal and, in some cases, to walls. |

The separation of paints into only two categories is somewhat crude and doesn't cover the host of hybrid paint types that were traditionally used. Many of these hybrid paints were mainly used in the art world rather than in the practice of painting houses, which is why I have not included a full discussion of them here.

Modern convention dictates that we need to cover timber with as many layers of paint as possible in order to protect it from the elements. This knowledge has been passed on from our grandparents to our parents to us and then on to our children over the past five to six decades. The problem with this approach is that water only needs a hairline crack in order to find its way into an object. It's completely natural for timber to expand and contract during the four seasons of the year as the temperature rises and falls, which means it's impossible to avoid these hairline cracks occurring. Once this water has made its way into the timber, it will then need to find its way out.

Unfortunately, the more coats of acrylic paint have been painted over the timber, the harder it will be

Flaking paint on a window.

for the water to get out again. In the best-case scenario, the water will then put pressure on the paint from within, causing it to flake and peel off. In the worst case, the layers of paint will be just too strong for the water to push through, so it will sit behind the paint instead, slowly saturating the timber. Once timber has become saturated underneath the paint, it will not be able to dry out, which will lead to rot. Timber wrapped in plastic petrochemical paint will always rot; it's just a matter of time.

## HOW DOES LINSEED PAINT WORK?

Linseed paint has a lower surface tension than water. This simple fact gives it two significant advantages over petrochemical, latex or acrylic paints:

- Linseed paint is able to penetrate deeper into timber than water ever will.
- Linseed paint has great 'wicking' properties.

Flaking paint on a siding.

Rotted timber behind modern paint.

The low surface tension of linseed paint allows it to do for timber what Gore-Tex® clothes do for us in a rainstorm. Raindrops are too large and have too high a surface tension to penetrate linseed oil paint, so rainwater beads off. However, water trapped in timber has a very small molecular size and the capillary action of the timber and linseed oil lets this moisture evaporate when air temperatures rise and air humidity drops. In short, linseed paint keeps water out for the main part, but it also lets any moisture that does get in evaporate out through the paint. This means that water never gets stuck under linseed paint, that timber never gets saturated from the inside and that any water escaping won't take flakes of paint with it.

The wicking aspect is less relevant when used on metal. In this case, the surface tension of the paint is far more important. Metal should be painted using linseed paint containing a haematite iron-oxide primer. This is because haematite has a lamellar (or scaly) structure, which prevents water penetration. In combination with the surface tension of linseed oil being lower than water, this means that the water cannot get

## HOW LINSEED PAINT WORKS ON TIMBER

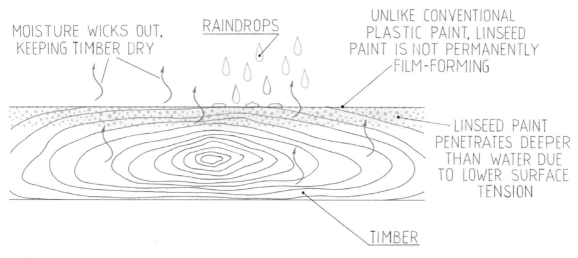

MOISTURE WICKS OUT, KEEPING TIMBER DRY

RAINDROPS

UNLIKE CONVENTIONAL PLASTIC PAINT, LINSEED PAINT IS NOT PERMANENTLY FILM-FORMING

LINSEED PAINT PENETRATES DEEPER THAN WATER DUE TO LOWER SURFACE TENSION

TIMBER

How linseed paint works on timber and other porous materials.

Old linseed paint in Drayton Hall near Charleston, South Carolina.

## A NOTE ON ROTTING TIMBER

The book *English Heritage Practical Building Conservation – Timber*, dedicates nearly a hundred pages to the effect of wood rot. It contains a huge amount of interesting information, but disappointingly there is no mention of the way that conventional plastic paint traps moisture in timber. Though the authors do state that they prefer to use linseed paint, the only reasoning they give for this is the fact that the maintenance cycle is longer: linseed paint can be left for five or more years before maintenance is needed, while plastic paint will need attention every two to three years.[22]

Quite simply, timber that stays dry does not rot. Though linseed paint can play a significant role in keeping timber dry, the environment the timber is in obviously also has an effect. If the relative air humidity is high and is coupled with a low temperature, the conditions for rot will be just about perfect. This is explored in the book *Timber Decay in Buildings and its Treatment*, though again the focus of this book is pretty much solely on treating the symptoms of rot rather than methods for preventing it in the first place.[23]

to the metal. Linseed paint and metal are discussed in more detail below and in Chapter 8.

### Is linseed paint breathable?

Having wicking properties is different from a paint being breathable. Linseed paint should not be classed as a breathable paint. Breathability implies two-way traffic, that water can move freely in and out through the paint. There are some paints, such as lime paint, that allow this to happen. However, linseed paint does not work this way.

Linseed paint is excellent at repelling water and keeping it out. However, as discussed earlier, water only needs a hairline crack to find its way in through a painted surface. The wicking properties of linseed paint act as an efficient second defence against any moisture that does find its way in.

## MOULD AND ALGAE GROWTH

Rot is not the only thing you may wish to protect your surface against. Algae and mould can both occur frequently, especially outside.

Algae is a green film that can form on any surface that stays wet for a prolonged period. Though it might not look very attractive, it is harmless as it is not toxic to either humans or adults. It will also have no adverse effect on the paint or the surface beneath. In most cases, it is relatively easy to wash off with soap and water.

Mould, however, is a different story. It produces mould spores that are easily breathed in and can then attack our immune system and cause inflammatory and autoimmune conditions. There is plenty of new

Algae on paint.

research coming out on this, but institutions like the Cleveland Clinic have proved this to be the case without doubt.[24] This subject matter is gaining a lot more understanding and becoming more mainstream in the UK and the USA, but, as usual, Scandinavian countries

Mould on white paint.

have made much bigger strides forwards in tackling the issue. This is explored further in Chapter 11.

## Why does mould occur?

If mould appears, the reason for its presence should always be investigated, especially inside. Generally, mould is caused by a lack of ventilation or air circulation in combination with low temperatures. Low dew points turn air vapour into moisture, or air droplets. Because this happens at the dew point, mould is usually found on or around windows, or in the bottom corners of the room (usually just above skirting boards or trims).

Mould should be cleaned off using white vinegar. Then, the surface needs to be rinsed really well to ensure that no vinegar is left. Finally, the surface should be given a fresh coat of linseed paint.

### Does linseed paint protect against mould?

Linseed paint does help to protect against mould, as long as it includes the correct pigments. Zinc white is a very commonly used pigment in linseed paint and a big part of the reason for this is due to its natural anti-mould properties. In order to be effective at helping to prevent mould, the pigment zinc white needs to be added in the correct quantities and at the correct time during production. Pigments tend to interact with each other in different ways, so they need to be combined at source rather than mixed into the paint separately later. (This also helps to ensure colour consistency; if you stir zinc white into paint later on, it will tint the paint.) When purchasing linseed paint, it's wise to check the list of pigments that are included to ensure that it contains zinc white. For best results in this respect, linseed paint should contain 10–15 per cent zinc white.

Unfortunately, zinc white cannot prevent mould growth altogether, especially if the circumstances are less than ideal. If a surface never has time to fully dry out, particularly if it's horizontal with standing water or never gets any direct sunlight, you may find that mould will occur. In these cases, the surface should be washed using white vinegar and then given a fresh coat of linseed paint.

## Does linseed paint protect against termites?

Linseed paint does not specifically repel termites. However, it does often help to keep them at bay. This is because linseed paint helps to keep timber dry, which makes it far less appealing to termites. In general, termites are attracted to damp or wet timber as it offers easier access and much better nourishment for them, though, of course, there are some exceptions to this rule.

# USING LINSEED PAINT ON METAL SURFACES

Though we often focus on how well linseed paint works on timber, it should not be overlooked that it also works well on metal. When working with a metal surface, it is less the paint's wicking properties and more its water-repellent qualities that make linseed paint an exceptionally good choice. The explanation for this is clear: the better that metal surfaces are protected from water, the better they will be protected from rust.

Though there are quite a number of publications dealing with the treatment of heritage ferrous structures, most do not cover linseed paint. Even if they do, readers are rarely given a convincing argument for its use. Luckily, there are plenty of examples out in the real world that show how well the anti-corrosive properties of linseed paint work on metal substrates, particularly iron. One of the most iconic must surely be the Sydney Harbour Bridge. Records show that

paint manufacturers Lewis Berger and Sons supplied 272,762ltr of linseed paint for the Sydney Harbour Bridge when it was built in 1932.[25]

In fact, pretty much any iron or steel construction built between the Industrial Revolution and World War II would have been painted with linseed paint. Usually, this paint would incorporate iron oxide and, possibly, aluminium pigment. This is true for large constructions such as bridges as well as railings, gates and even trains. Many of these structures are still in excellent condition – and regular use – today.

## How does linseed paint protect metal?

While the benefit of using linseed paint on timber is related to the paint's wicking properties, this is obviously not the case with metal. Rather, the benefit of using linseed paint on metal lies in the paint's ability to prevent water coming into direct contact with the surface of the metal.

As stated earlier in this chapter, paint should be considered first and foremost as a sacrificial layer to protect the surface on which it is painted from the elements, including both moisture and UV light. This is even more important for metal surfaces, as linseed paint cannot penetrate metal in order to provide further protection. Instead, protecting the surface is completely dependent on the strength of the paint layer, as when this begins to deteriorate, the metal beneath is at risk of water exposure. Water exposure, of course, can cause rust and corrosion, which can have very serious implications for structures such as roofs, bridges and walkways.

It is important to protect metal structures from rust and corrosion from a safety perspective, but also from an environmental one. There is no reason why metal structures cannot last indefinitely with the right treatment and ongoing care. Though metal is not necessarily a hugely environmentally sustainable material in itself, if we look at things from a life-cycle point of view, many of the ferrous structures still in use today have already paid off much, if not all, of their debts in

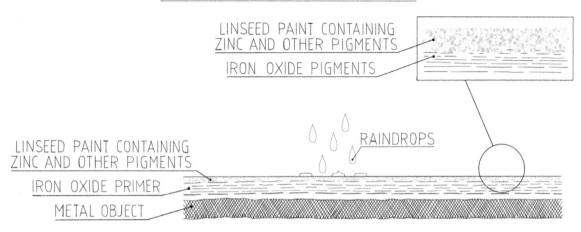

## HOW LINSEED PAINT WORKS ON METAL

LINSEED PAINT CONTAINING
ZINC AND OTHER PIGMENTS

IRON OXIDE PIGMENTS

RAINDROPS

LINSEED PAINT CONTAINING
ZINC AND OTHER PIGMENTS

IRON OXIDE PRIMER

METAL OBJECT

How linseed paint works on metal.

terms of the carbon footprints used to manufacture them. By ensuring that these structures continue to be cared for and are regularly maintained with linseed paint, we can reduce the amount of ferrous metals that need to be produced in the future. This idea is covered in more detail in Arja Källbom's seminal PhD thesis, *Painting Treatments of Weather-Exposed Ferrous Heritage*.[26]

## Chapter Four

# A Short Guide to Pigments and Colours

## Function Over Form

In their work on Colonial Williamsburg, Carson and Lounsbury mention the following:

> At first, finishes were primarily functional and were used to protect vulnerable surfaces, generally with natural tar-based coatings that provided a measure of weatherproofing but not much more ... Gradually, changing expectations and the increasing supply of a wider range of pigments, binders and varnishes allowed for a host of new ways to protect and decorate the houses of the colonies' wealthiest residents.[27]

Function always comes first. Linseed paint is perennially popular because its moisture-wicking properties keep timber dry, and dry timber does not rot. However, even though colour is – and always should be – of secondary importance, the psychology behind it is indisputable. Historically, colour has always been linked to social status. To see this, one only has to look at the traditional canal green (or *grachtengroen*) doors of the wealthy Dutch merchants in Amsterdam, or King Gustav of Sweden's drive to imitate the red brick buildings of Holland's Golden Age, which resulted in the emergence of oxide-red barns all over Sweden.

Different colours combined with different lighting can have a profound effect on our state of mind. Many books have been written about colour analysis and historical colours, but the main work on this subject is *Theory of Colours* by Johann Wolfgang von Goethe in the nineteenth century. Along with Goethe, many scholars throughout history have attempted to interpret colour and standardise it, including Claude Boutet, Tobias Mayer, Moses Harris, Ignaz Schifmüller, James Sowerby, David Hay, Aemillus Müller, Charles Hayter and Abraham Gottlob Werner. In addition to the myriad theoretical works that have been written on the subject, many independent manufacturers and organisations have also sought to develop standards, including Munsell, Ridgeway, Benjamin Moore, Dulux, The British Standard, RAL and NCS.

In 1692, the Dutch artist A. Boogert arguably created the very first colour standard in his guide, *Klaer Lightende Spiegel der Verfkonst* (which translates roughly as 'clear shining mirror of the art of painting'). In this one-off, 900-page, handwritten work, Boogert approaches colour in a scientific way. He presents a number of shades and tints of each main colour by mixing them. Since the printing press in those days did not have the capability to reproduce this work, there was only one copy. This original manuscript found its way to the Bibliothèque Méjanes in Aix-en-Provence,

*Klaer Lightende Spiegel der Verfkonst.*

France, in 1916, donated by a French palaeographic archivist. The Spanish publisher Galobart Books digitised and printed the work in 2021, which has allowed people to rediscover this treasure.[28]

Though there is undoubtedly a great deal of interest in colour and its historical context, here I will bring the focus back to the importance of form over function. As interesting as the microscopic analysis of paint colour is, it becomes irrelevant if that colour is then recreated using a modern plastic or petrochemical alternative. After all, a piece of timber does not care what colour it gets painted or oiled in. All it requires is the correct kind of nourishment: one that will keep it dry without suffocating it. In truth, if the correct ingredients are used, the character of the final colour will always be in line with the historical values.

Despite this, a whole industry has been created around historical paint analysis, only for the resulting colours to be mixed in modern emulsions and gloss paints. Even some highly regarded scholars have built a brand around their historical colour expertise, just to then team up with modern manufacturers. What is the point of investing time and money in accurate historical research, only to wrap the recipient fabric in the equivalent of a plastic bag? The colours used as part of these so-called 'historical ranges' may be right, but the chemical make-up of the paint is certainly not correct for the structure of the building. Once again: function really must come before form.

Of course, there's a good argument to say that colour is a completely subjective experience, making this whole practice largely irrelevant. As Joseph Albers states in *Interaction of Color*:

… it is hard, if not impossible, to remember distinct colors … Even if all the [listeners] have hundreds of reds in front of them from which to choose the Coca-Cola red, they will … select quite different colors. And no one can be sure that he has found the precise red shade.[29]

With this in mind, we will leave the psychological colour analysis to the theorists. Instead, we will focus on

pigments and their actual practical properties. This is a fascinating topic and choosing the correct pigments can actually make a lot of difference in terms of wood preservation. To clarify, when we talk about pigments, we're referring to the powder pigments that form the basis of linseed paint. Colourants used in a tinting machine are petrochemical derivatives, which will not be discussed here as they have no place in the production of natural, historically accurate paint.

## The Role of Pigments

The most valuable information about pigments can be found in:

- *The Chemistry of Paints and Painting* by Arthur Herbert Church (1890)
- *Painters' Colors, Oils and Varnishes: A Practical Manual* by George H. Hurst (1892)
- *The Mixing of Colors and Paints* by F.N. Vanderwalker (1924)
- *Painting and Decorating* by A.E. Hurst (1963).

In *The Chemistry of Paints and Painting*, Arthur Herbert Church published a table grouping pigments in terms of their stability in oil paints (pp. 226–7), which still stands today.[30]

If we remove toxic pigments and those unsuitable for use with linseed oil and add in the more recently discovered stable pigments, we are left with the reworked model shown in the table opposite.

Following Church's classification, we will approach the pigments in the chronological order in which they were first used. We will focus on non-toxic, opaque pigments. This, therefore, excludes some traditional pigments, such as arsenic.

### Blacks

Black, specifically bone black and carbon black, can be considered the mother of all pigments. Both these

## Pigments suitable for use in linseed oil paint

| Brown and black |
| --- |
| Burnt sienna |
| Brown umber |
| Verona brown |
| Carbon black |
| Bone black |
| Graphite |
| Van Dyke brown (earthy version) |

| Yellow |
| --- |
| Yellow ochre |
| Raw sienna |
| Cadmium yellow |
| Chrome yellow |

| Red |
| --- |
| Vermillion |
| Venetian red |
| Red ochre |

| White |
| --- |
| Zinc white |
| Titanium white* |
| Lead white** |
| Lithopone |

| Green |
| --- |
| Green oxide |
| Green umber |
| Green earth |
| Viridian |

| Blue |
| --- |
| Ultramarine |
| Cobalt |
| Cerulean |
| Prussian blue |

* Not available in Church's time, but a very stable and solid white pigment that is often used.
** Very toxic and should be avoided; included because of the historical context of linseed paint.

organic pigments date back to prehistoric times. They are relatively slow drying due to being made from organic matter. In more recent times, synthetic black pigments have been made from natural gas deposits (lamp black), as well as by burning wine lees (which results in a bluish black).

### Bone black

Bone black is made from burnt animal bone (or, historically, ivory) and produces the deepest available black pigment. It absorbs a lot of light, which is what makes it appear so dark.

### Graphite

Graphite is a really interesting mineral pigment, as it is an earthy version of carbon black. It occurs naturally in geological areas that have been subject to extreme temperature exposure. When it was first discovered in the sixteenth century in Seathwaite, England, it was initially mistaken for lead because of its colour.[31]

### Carbon black

Carbon black (or charcoal) is the sister of bone black, made from burnt plants and wood. It is not quite

Bone black.

Graphite.

Carbon black.

earth pigment (very often made from peat), the modern-day version is made using asphaltum black and iron oxide.

## Yellows

### Yellow ochre

The ochres followed very closely on the heels of bone and carbon black. Broadly speaking, they come in two versions: yellow and red. The use of both yellow and red ochres dates back as far as the early Egyptians and Etruscans. Traces of these have been found in cave paintings tens of thousands of years old in the Altamira Caves in Bilbao, Spain, as well as the Lascaux Caves in Montignac, France, and the Blombos Cave on the southern cape of South Africa.

Yellow and red ochres are very closely related and are both very ferric (meaning that they contain a lot of iron). The only real difference between them relates to how they 'hold' water, or, more specifically, how water molecules chemically bind to them.

Yellow ochre is found all over the world. Unsurprisingly, this means that it comes in a lot of different

as deep in colour as bone black, with more of an anthracite hue.

### Van Dyke brown

Van Dyke brown (named after the famous Dutch artist) is also sometimes called Cassel or Cologne earth, as it resembles these local pigments in colour. Though Van Dyke brown was originally an organic

Yellow ochre.

hues. Because the quality of natural yellow ochre varied so much and therefore could not be relied upon, synthetic versions found their way to the market quite early on. When heated (either by way of burning or calcinating), yellow ochre starts turning pink (known as light red), then turns red and, finally, a deep purplish brown.

## Raw sienna

Raw sienna is another primaeval raw earth pigment that was used by the earliest humans. It is a brownish-yellow pigment found in and around Siena, Italy, where it began to be produced on a much larger scale by artists during the Renaissance. When calcined, the pigment develops into a darker brown, known as burnt sienna. Sienna has a reasonably high manganese content, which means that it helps to reduce the drying time of any oil with which it is mixed.

## Synthetic yellows

The problem of unstable and widely varying yellow ochres meant that there was a huge demand for synthetic alternatives. A range of oxide yellows was developed in response, using a variety of different production methods. However, the various impurities that are included in the process mean that even synthetic yellow pigments can be very temperamental in terms of hue and quality. The most common oxide yellows are chrome yellow and cadmium yellow.

## Chrome yellow

Louis Nicolas Vauquelin first extracted chrome yellow from the mineral crocoite in 1797 and managed to produce a man-made version by 1804. It took another decade and a half before it became commercially available. Chrome yellow was a bit of a revelation for the art market of the day. The pigment dispersed well in water and oil and was relatively lightfast. It also provided great coverage and vibrancy. However, it did have a habit of darkening over time when exposed to UV light, which meant that it wasn't usable as a house paint (unless it was mixed with Prussian blue, which created a relatively bright and stable green). Another major flaw of chrome yellow was that it turned out to be highly toxic.

Raw sienna.

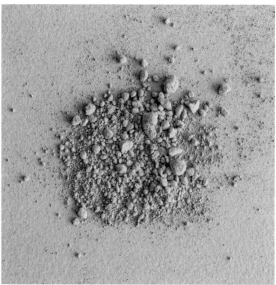

Chrome yellow.

### Cadmium yellow

Cadmium yellow was first synthesised in 1817 by Friedrich Stromeyer. It gives a warm yellow to orange hue. Cadmium is a very stable pigment in linseed oil and offers good permanence and tinting power. It can be harmful to people in large quantities, but is safe in the quantities needed to mix with linseed oil.

## Reds

### Red ochre

Red ochre is one of the abundant earth pigments. Essentially, it is rust-stained clay and is found all over the world. Just like yellow ochre, the fact that red ochre is so commonly found worldwide means that it comes in many different shades. In its raw form, some types of red ochre can appear grey or even black until they are finely ground and reveal their typical cherry-red hue. Towards the middle of the nineteenth century, synthetic versions of red ochre began to replace the original natural pigments.

All red ochres are lightfast and are known for being exceptionally durable. When mixed with linseed oil, the haematite iron oxide from Bilbao, Spain, has particularly good anti-rust properties. By observing the haematite under a microscope, you can see that it has a reasonably scaly surface. When combined with linseed oil, which has low surface tension, this scaliness provides a coating that simply does not allow any moisture through. Painting metal with this combination therefore prevents rust.

### Venetian red

Venetian red is a naturally occurring red ochre. It is found all over the world, which means that it can, therefore, vary enormously in colour, just like the abundantly occurring yellow ochre. This variation means that Venetian red is known by quite a few

Venetian red.

other names, including terra rosa, Tuscan red, Indian red and light English red. This pigment is very stable in linseed oil, though it tends to need longer drying times than some other pigments.

### Vermillion

Traditionally, vermillion was made by grinding cinnabar, a naturally occurring mineral pigment. Cinnabar is mostly found in Spain, but also in other parts of Europe, China, Japan, California, Mexico and Peru. In its powder form, vermillion is usually scarlet or red. Vermillion was previously known by the names vermiculous, cannabaris cenobrium and minium, which is still used by some older trades. In the absence of cinnabar, vermillion can also be made by combining sulphur and mercury. Historically, this combination would be cut with red lead, which led to people calling it 'red lead paint'.

When used in linseed oil, vermillion, or cinnabar, does not dry particularly well. However, the colour is very stable. Indeed, the paintings *The Painter and his Pug* by William Hogarth (1745) and *Mary Sidney, Countess of Pembroke* by Marcus Gheeraerts (1614) both contain vermillion and still look great today. Both can be seen in the National Portrait Gallery, London.

Iron-oxide haematite red.

## Burnt umber

Burnt umber is made by heating umber, a reddish-brown earth pigment containing iron and manganese oxide compounds. It is, of course, the presence of iron that gives this pigment its red hue. The higher the percentage, typically the richer the tint. This colour can be enhanced by calcining or burning the raw umber to create burnt umber.

Burnt brown umber.

Burnt umber mixes reasonably well with other pigments. It offers good tinting strength and great opacity. Thanks to its manganese content, it helps oil to dry more quickly and forms a good, flexible film.

## Whites

Though earth whites, such as chalk and gypsum, disperse very well in water-based mediums, they do not work in linseed oil. This is because the refractive index is very similar to that of the oil, making it look semi-translucent. However, metal-based whites, such as lead white and zinc white, disperse really well in linseed oil. Both of these pigments give excellent coverage and opacity.

## Lead white

Lead white is the only toxic metal pigment we will focus on here, and for very good reason. Historically, lead white was the primary metal-based white. Even nowadays, people still refer to 'lead paint', when they actually mean linseed paint with lead white as the main ingredient. We know that it has been used since ancient times, as face-powder remnants containing lead white dating from around 400BC have been found near Athens, Greece. Practically speaking, lead white in linseed oil is exceptionally durable, particularly for surfaces that are exposed to the weather. However, it does have a tendency to yellow relatively quickly and change the character of the colour in which it has been used.

Several different methods were used to produce lead white. Most were deceptively simple, but all of them were hazardous to the health of the workers involved in the process. In the oldest technique, known as the Dutch stack method, lead sheets were rolled into a coil or spiral, then exposed to vinegar fumes (sometimes the vinegar was combined with dung fumes). In later times, the vinegar was replaced with acetic acid, carbonic acid and water vapour in order to speed up the process. In both methods, once the sheets were ready, they would be unfolded and the white flakes that had developed on them would be collected up. These flakes were then mixed with water and pressed together to form a compact cake. This cake could then be ground to the desired grain size.

Lead exposure was known to be very dangerous for centuries before the pigment fell out of regular use. Workers responsible for processing lead, as well as painters and decorators who worked with the powder, were often diagnosed with lead poisoning. This could cause serious and irreversible mental illness, as well as anaemia, infertility and even death.

### Zinc white, or zinc oxide (ZnO)

Though the risks of working with lead white had been known for centuries, according to Church, the use of carbonate of zinc instead was only suggested for the first time by Monsieur Courtois and Louis-Bernard Guyton de Morveau at L'Académie de Dijon, France, in 1787. There do appear to be some earlier mentions of this suggestion, but they are almost exclusively in the context of art and painting rather than a building application. Whoever first made the suggestion, it is believed that zinc white was not used at all before the 1850s, which can prove very useful

Zinc white.

when trying to date historical paint finishes. Zinc white is very easy to identify as it fluoresces brightly under ultraviolet light.

In terms of safety, zinc white has clear benefits over lead white and is an obvious first choice to use as a white pigment. Just like lead white, zinc white contains properties that help to prevent mould growth. However, it tends to dry significantly quicker in linseed oil than its toxic equivalent, which can lead to cracking and chalking. It also does not have quite the same lasting power as lead white, though it is still very opaque and durable, especially when combined with titanium dioxide.

Thanks to its anti-mould properties, most linseed paints should contain zinc white. If your linseed paint doesn't, it's possible to add it yourself, though do keep in mind that you need a roller mill and it will affect the final tint of the colour.

### Lithopone

Chronologically, lithopone was used between zinc oxide and titanium dioxide. It was discovered in the 1870s and, at the time, was one of the most effective white pigments available. It produced far better coverage than lead white and zinc white, and even retained a certain flexibility.

However, lithopone does have a significant downside, in that it becomes blackened when exposed to UV light. This, of course, makes it pretty much useless for exterior applications, as the colour does not remain stable when exposed to sunlight. This is a significant part of the reason why lithopone is not in common use today (and why I do not put it in my paints at Brouns & Co). The other reason that lithopone is not used as widely today is because of the easy availability of titanium white.

### Titanium white, or titanium dioxide (TiO$_2$)

Titanium white is one of the more modern pigments used in linseed paint. Though it was first discovered in 1821, it was not until much later that the technology

Titanium white.

pigments was rendered obsolete once Prussian blue came on the market. It is important to take into account that blue pigments can behave erratically in linseed oil, which means that blue architectural linseed paint is not always colour-stable.

### Ultramarine blue

In his *Book of the Arts*, written around 1400, Cennino Cennini described ultramarine as 'A noble colour, beautiful, the most perfect of all colours.' The original ultramarine was derived from ground lapis lazuli. This semi-precious stone is found on almost all continents, but is historically linked with Sar-e Sang in the Koksha Valley in Afghanistan, where the highest quality lapis-lazuli gems are still found today.

If available and affordable, the pigment was a great choice to use with linseed oil as it was very stable, did not fade and had excellent opacity. The lazurite present in the gem is what gives it, and the ultramarine pigment derived from it, the gorgeous, deep-blue colour. The Medici were known to be big fans of lapis lazuli and incorporated the gem and the colour into a lot of their ornamental pieces. Tutankhamun's death mask has an inlay of glass and lapis lazuli.

to mass-produce it became available. The pigment was first commercially produced for industrial purposes in Norway in 1916, then in 1921 the first colour suitable for artistic purposes was introduced by an American manufacturer.[32]

Titanium white is not as brilliantly white as zinc white, but it offers great durability and opacity. Though it does still dry very quickly, it gives a much more elastic finish than zinc white. Mixing the two pigments together in linseed oil can create a very strong, protective finish that combines the durability and opacity of titanium white with the brilliance and anti-mould properties of zinc white.

### Blues

In the past, blue pigment was used rarely and usually only for specific applications, such as fine art. This is because the naturally occurring blue pigments, azurite and lapis lazuli, were made from semi-precious stones that were difficult to source and therefore expensive. (Other blue pigments such as indigo, woad blue and blue verditer were available, but these did not work particularly well in combination with linseed oil.) The use of azurite and lapis lazuli as paint

Ultramarine blue.

Lapis lazuli in Tutankhamun's death mask.

sustainable, and the Société d'Encouragement pour l'Industrie Nationale in Paris, France, held a competition in 1824, offering a prize to the first person who could create a synthetic alternative to ultramarine blue. Interestingly, though a man named Jean-Baptiste Guimet managed this in 1826, he kept his findings secret and the competition was won by Christian Gmelin in 1828.

### Prussian blue

At some point between 1706 and 1710 (scholars have varying opinions on this), Johann Jacob Diesbach invented Prussian blue by accident. He was working in his lab in Berlin, trying to create an artificial version of cochineal dye. By the mid-1700s, Prussian blue (or Berlin blue, as it is sometimes called) was the most widely used blue pigment, thanks to its stability and affordability

However, even Prussian blue will not maintain a consistent shade in linseed paint over time. When Prussian blue is suspended in linseed oil, the oil makes the pigment appear much darker. Once the paint is applied and exposed to UV light, the linseed oil will slowly be stripped away, revealing the true colour

Though the colour and opacity of ultramarine blue are certainly very attractive, unfortunately the pigment can react strongly to mineral acids. Mineral acids are present in most earth and mineral pigments, which means that when ultramarine is mixed with these other pigments, over time the bold blue will develop into a washed-out mid-grey.

This was the case on the Chatsworth Estate, where a previous paint mixture had combined ultramarine blue with oxide black and titanium oxide. Though the colour this produced had initially been the perfect 'Chatsworth Blue', after a few years the mineral acids in the oxide black and titanium oxide faded the ultramarine to grey. This is just one example of why an understanding of pigment interaction is so important when mixing colours with linseed oil. It is also the reason you will not find ultramarine blue in many types of good quality modern linseed paint.

By the seventeenth century, the price of lapis lazuli was equivalent to that of gold.[33] This was clearly not

Prussian blue.

of the raw pigment. This usually occurs after a few years of exposure, when the surface painted with the blue linseed paint will take on a slightly green or turquoise hue.

### Cobalt blue

Sometimes also referred to as smalt blue, cobalt blue is another synthetic invention by a French entrepreneur. It was created in 1802 by Louis Jacques Thénard.

Cobalt blue is a very stable pigment created by heating a mixture of cobalt chloride and aluminium oxide. The result is a pigment with a lighter, more violet hue than ultramarine blue or Prussian blue. Moreover, it suspends beautifully in linseed oil and is unaffected by UV light, moisture or oxygen.

### Cerulean blue

Cerulean is not a naturally occurring pigment. Rather, it is made from cobalt magnesium stannate. It was a latecomer to the pigment market, first introduced in the mid-1800s. The main benefit of cerulean blue is that it is lightfast.

## Browns

### Burnt sienna

As mentioned earlier, burnt sienna is produced by burning raw sienna. During the burning process, the raw sienna first turns from yellow to a reddish brown (usually when it reaches around 60°C). If it is burnt for longer, it continues to develop into a deeper, darker brown.

Sienna contains a relatively large proportion of manganese (about 5 per cent), which aids drying. This means that adding burnt sienna to other pigments in linseed oil can make the resulting paint dry faster. Burnt sienna can also reduce the intensity of other colours and make them appear older and more faded.

Burnt sienna.

### Brown umber

Like sienna and ochre, brown umber is an earth pigment, which means that it comes in an almost infinite number of shades, though it is typically browner and darker than burnt sienna. Different varieties can be imported from all over the world, including France, Cyprus and Germany. Each type has slightly different properties, which can be put to different uses.

Brown umber has excellent opacity. It is also one of the most durable colours; anything painted using a brown umber should stay good for many years without any noticeable degradation.

## Greens

### Green oxide

Green oxide, also known as chromium green oxide, is a relatively new pigment, introduced in the mid-1800s. It may have been available before then as an artist pigment, but it only became available for architectural paints around 1850. Like many other man-made pigments, green oxide was invented in France.

Chromium green oxide.

Green umber.

The main benefit of green oxide was that it was more stable than the copper greens, which meant that it had replaced most other green pigments by the 1870s.[34]

### Green umber

Green umber is an absolute favourite for us with linseed paint thanks to its stability in linseed oil and its excellent tinting strength. It is a real, raw earth pigment, composed of natural earth and iron oxide. It has an olive-brown appearance.

### Green earth

Green earth (also known as terre verte) comprises glauconite and celadonite, which are mineral pigments found in rock deposits. The highest quality versions tend to come from Bentonico, near Verona, Italy, though it can be found in various parts of Europe and the Americas. Use of this pigment stretches right back to Roman times – traces have been found on murals and paintings in Pompeii. However, green earth is not an effective pigment to use with linseed oil as the resulting mixture produces a translucent paint.

### Viridian, or chromium oxide

Viridian is also known as Spanish green and copper green. It is made from the minerals copper diacetate, copper dioxide and copper dicarbonate. Though the pigment is an attractive blue-toned green, it does not have great opacity on its own. For this reason, historically it was often mixed with lead white or yellow ochre.

Spanish green was one of the pigments used to create the famous *grachtengroen*, or canal green, doors in Amsterdam. Recent analysis by Ron Nieuwenhuis, the head of restoration of Diogenes, has shown that Spanish green was used in combination with linseed oil and yellow ochre to create the brighter green *grachtengroen* hue found on Oude Waal, which dates from 1725.[35]

## Mixing Pigments

This chapter contains only a taster of the many available pigments, but hopefully it will make clear that each pigment has its own unique properties. In order to mix pigments successfully and develop new shades, it is important to understand how pigments will interact with each other.

Here we come back to the question of function over form. Mixing base colour pigments can produce attractive new shades and colours, but this cannot be done without considering the resulting balance of properties. For example:

- adding an umber can improve drying times, while adding black can slow them down
- adding zinc white can help combat mould growth, but when not properly balanced with other pigments it can make the paint dry too quickly, causing it to crack
- adding Prussian blue or ultramarine can give real depth of colour, but can affect the durability of the paint when exposed to UV light.

As a general rule, adding white through to red and the other primary colours to a base colour creates tints, whilst adding black through to green to primary colours creates shades. The most visually attractive colours usually contain both.

To be successful, the process of mixing pigments with linseed oil can involve a measure of trial and error. A good mix will produce an attractive paint that, more importantly, suits the surface it is being painted on and will protect it for many years to come.

## How linseed paint is mixed

Traditionally, artists and decorators made their own paints by mixing a paste from their chosen pigments and an oil base. They would do this by using simple, manual tools – just a glass muller (a short-handled tool for grinding pigments) and a slab. They would start by grinding the powder pigments with a little bit of oil, then would add more oil as necessary to create the correct consistency. Artists would typically use less oil in their paint, while house painters would use more in order to create a thinner paint more suited for painting over large areas.

Dosing the pigment.

Readying the pigment.

Adding the boiled oil.

Though this technique no doubt worked for centuries, it is not the most effective way to make paint. Not only is it time-consuming and labour-intensive, it is also quite difficult to produce a consistent result

Mixing the boiled oil and powder pigment.

Grinding the pigment.

Paint ready to use.

Pigment completely dispersed.

each time. To ensure the durability of the paint, it is essential for the linseed oil and the pigments to be fully amalgamated with each other. If the paint is not properly mixed, it will go matt far more quickly, which will increase the requirements for maintenance.

In order to achieve this nowadays, paint manufacturers use column mixers and big barrels. The paint that is mixed in these barrels will then be transferred to a triple roller mill.

Here, the paint, which has more of a paste consistency at this stage, will pass through the rollers three to five times, depending on the grain size of the pigments used. This process creates a beautifully homogeneous consistency, which forms the basis for the eventual paint colours. It is important to note, however, that the mixture needs to stay at room temperature. The friction of metal on metal generates considerable heat and if the oil gets too hot it will become thinner, which makes it more difficult for the pigment to tack to it. This means that the milling process needs to involve additional measures to keep the oil and paste at the right temperature. This is achieved by using rollers that have a constant flow of cool water inside them.

Setting aside the modern machines and additional cooling techniques, in principle the method we use today of grinding pigment into boiled oil is hundreds of years old. With this in mind, you can begin to understand why linseed paint is more expensive to produce than modern plastic paint. This should also give you a clear idea of what to expect from a high-quality linseed paint supplier.

## A note on colour matching

There is a whole industry of paint analysts waiting to analyse historical paint samples for renovators. These analysts will examine samples on a microscopic level in order to date renovation projects and give an approximation of what the original colour would have looked like. This can certainly be helpful in some situations, especially if you're seeking to return an important historical building as close as possible to its original decor. However, the problem with these practices is that colour perception will only ever be an approximation. This is especially true if the colour references the analysts come up with are then taken to the local DIY shop to be mixed up in modern plastic paint.

It is important to remember that linseed oil is a natural product and as such it has natural variations in colour. When it is mixed with pigments, the exact hue of the oil will have an impact on the final colour, which is a factor that cannot be accounted for by paint analysts. In other words, there is no way to know the exact shade that would have been used in a project.

Personally, I believe it is far more important to attempt to match the ingredients of the original paint, including both the pigments *and* the historically accurate paint itself, as this will enable you to match the overall feel and character of the original decor. This simply cannot be achieved with plastic or petrochemical paints, no matter the brand or how clever the styling of their adverts.

Barrel mixer.

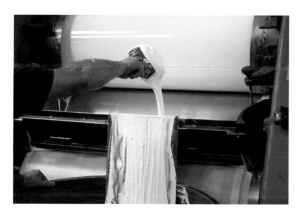

Feeding the triple roller mill.

Paint coming out of the mill.

## Chapter Five

# A Short Guide to Timber

Looking at modern building practices, you could be forgiven for thinking that timber was not a strong, long-lasting building material in its own right. Today's architects and building industry professionals seem to gravitate towards man-made or 'enhanced' materials, including engineered and hybrid timbers. This seems a strange choice, when there are all kinds of facts and, more importantly, precedents, that show the strength and durability of timber. From the Kondō at Hōryū-ji in Nara, Japan, and the Great Hall of Foguang Temple in Mount Wutai, China, to the Stål-ekleivloftet in Eidsborg, Norway, and the Fairbanks House in Massachusetts, USA, there are numerous examples all over the northern hemisphere of softwood standing the test of time.

A quick search on the Internet will tell you that all of these buildings are hundreds of years old and that they still consist mainly of the original timbers. The reason for this is undoubtedly because the softwoods used in the construction of these buildings have never been treated with coatings or paints that trap moisture. Precedent and science are both clear on this fact – timber degrades when moisture becomes trapped in it. By choosing to avoid the types of paints, coatings and treatments that trap moisture, we can vastly prolong the lifespan of timber.

## THE DIFFERENCE BETWEEN HARDWOODS AND SOFTWOODS

Timber is generally split into two categories – hardwoods and softwoods. Though these terms have had different meanings in the past, they are now used in reference to the type of tree the timber has come from. It is important to note that the names 'hardwood' and 'softwood' can be misleading, as some softwoods can be harder than some hardwoods.

### Types of Hardwoods and Softwoods

| Hardwoods | Softwoods |
|---|---|
| Hardwoods are usually deciduous. They have broad leaves and bear flowers. | Softwoods are usually evergreen. They are coniferous trees. |
| Hardwoods include: | Softwoods include: |
| Beech<br>Ebony<br>Elm<br>Mahogany<br>Oak<br>Teak<br>Walnut | Fir<br>Pine<br>Spruce<br>Yew |

Though there are some clear differences between the types of trees that hardwoods and softwoods come from, the differences between the timber that comes from those trees is less easy to see. In fact, the important distinction between the two is at a microscopic level and is concerned with the structure of the fibres and how they interact with moisture. *The English Heritage Practical Building Conservation Guide on Timber* describes these structural differences as below:

Hardwood trees conduct water through elongated cells that overlap at their ends to form a column extending from the roots of the tree to its crown. The end walls between the cells break down into porous perforation plates which can trap any air bubbles that may form in the sap but allow water conduction to be more or less direct ... structural strength is applied by fibres which are long narrow cells with closed and pointed ends that do not conduct water.

Softwood trees are structured in a different fashion to the hardwoods. Both water conduction and strength are provided by one form of closed-ended cell, called a tracheid, and conduction between each cell and its neighbour is through valves ... The valves can close, trapping any air bubbles that form in the sap and would interfere with its conduction. Tracheids produce an indirect water transportation system that increases the tree's ability to cope with harsh environments.[36]

These structural differences are important in terms of linseed oil and petrochemical paint because they help to explain why different types of timber react differently to linseed. Because of their cell and fibre structure, softwoods are able to absorb linseed oil better, which allows the outer parts of the timber to be saturated with linseed paint.

## CHOOSING AN IDEAL SOFTWOOD

Just as there are key differences between hardwoods and softwoods, there are also many smaller differences among the various types of softwoods and even the different ages of softwoods. In many cases, there might not be much choice about what kind of timber to use. When you choose to use linseed paint, you will often be painting timber that has been in situ for quite some time. Though this may initially seem like a downside, reusing old timber is often a much better choice than replacing it with new for more reasons than just sustainability and the expense.

### The advantage of historical timber

It's important to understand that there is a noticeable difference between pine wood that was harvested before World War I and pine wood harvested after it. Harvesting practices changed significantly in the 1920s, with pine trees usually being cut down as soon as they reached harvesting age (approximately twenty years). This practice continues today, which is very different to before World War I, when pine trees would only have been cut down when they were much older (usually at least fifty years).[37] This shift is significant because younger trees have a much higher sap content, which makes them more vulnerable both to attacks from furniture beetles and to decay caused by dry rot. The higher heartwood content in older timber is clearly visible by the much denser growth rings (see image below).

It is for this reason that it is almost always better to restore existing slow-grown pine than to replace it with new timber. Most buildings dating from the Victorian era, the Georgian era and earlier will have used slow-grown pine. Not only is this the best timber to use in conjunction with linseed paint, it is also far more sustainable to use timber that is already in

Cross-section of old and new pine.

place in terms of environmental considerations and embodied energy.

## Is there a good modern alternative?

Of course, it is not always possible to use older timber. Even if you are involved in an historical renovation project, there will be times when new timber needs to be brought in. In these cases, a good alternative may be Douglas fir.

Thomas Drewett's PhD thesis, *The Growth and Quality of UK-Grown Douglas-Fir*, confirms increasing anecdotal evidence that Douglas fir is an excellent softwood for use as a building material. Drewett specifically evaluates timber grown in UK soil and climatic conditions, but considering that it is native to the north-western Pacific regions of America and Canada, it is hardly surprising to see the species performs so well in tests.[38] Drewett's conclusion is that:

> Douglas fir is a highly valued timber species in the UK that is likely to be more suitable in a range of sites with a forecast increased climate scenario. Stronger, stiffer and denser than the most commercially important timber species currently grown (Sitka spruce) in the UK, Douglas fir has the potential to supply the end-user with a durable and, at a minimum, comparably graded timber material. While Douglas fir is not a potential 'like for like' (in grading terms) replacement for imported C24 pine and spruce, it does grade well with acoustic grading machines, meaning it has potential for small volume grading by sawmills using portable grading machines (e.g., Brookhuis MTG). Douglas fir has the ability to continue producing quality timber for the UK in the future.[39]

A strong, durable and – perhaps most importantly – natural timber like Douglas fir will work brilliantly with linseed paint.

Douglas fir.

## The importance of using dried, aged timber

If you are using new timber for a project, it is important to make sure that you choose timber that has dried and aged. This kind of timber really will produce the best results in terms of getting a good finish with linseed paint and, more importantly, longevity.

When they are alive, all trees, be they hardwood or softwood, carry sap from their roots up through the trunk and out along their branches to the leaves. The sap is carried through the 'outer part of the woody stem,'[40] known as the sapwood. Once a tree has been cut down, the sapwood will begin to die. This is a slow process, as it takes time for the sap and resins from the sapwood to dry out. If timber is used before this process is complete, the remaining moisture will likely compromise the strength of the wood and the effectiveness of the linseed paint. The process of the sapwood dying off can be accelerated by kiln-drying the timber.

Cross-section showing heartwood, sapwood and bark
(from right to left).

## WHAT ABOUT HARDWOODS?

Though it is true that softwoods take linseed paint more effectively than hardwoods, that does not mean that it can't be used with hardwoods. There may be a particular reason why hardwood is the best choice of timber for a particular project, or you may be making use of whatever timber is already in place or is available to you.

### Hardwoods and petrochemical paints

When petrochemical, film-forming paints were introduced in the 1940s, it created a demand for more stable, less absorbent surfaces. The paint industry began advocating for the use of exotic hardwoods, along with man-made materials such as uPVC.

Hardwoods were popular for use with petrochemical paints because their less-absorbent nature often resulted in a better finish. However, this finish tended to be short-lived, as petrochemical paints would trap any moisture within the hardwood and, after a season or two, this would result in peeling paint. Interestingly, even relatively young wood could still bleed sap or resin and the film-forming character of the plastic paints would stop that sap from passing through the paint to the surface, leading to long-term damage to the wood.

### Using linseed paint on hardwoods

As linseed paint does not form a film or trap moisture, it may not come as a surprise to hear that painting exotic hardwoods with linseed paint can be difficult. In particular, relatively freshly cut, high resinous timber can keep bleeding for several years and in these cases the sap can therefore pass through linseed paint.

If you are considering using linseed paint on a hardwood, the age of the wood is crucial. Historical hardwood that has fully dried out can work really well with linseed paint. Mahogany that is roughly 100 years old (or younger mahogany that has been properly dried out) works particularly well.

### A note on hybrid timbers

In the mid to late 2000s, the building industry's decades-long interest in exotic hardwoods and man-made materials spawned the development of hybrid timbers. These are often referred to as 'engineered' timbers. In these, timber is still the main component, but man-made interventions have changed it from a low-carbon, natural building material to something less natural.

One example is Accoya, a brand name for radiata pine, a fast-growing softwood timber grown on wood farms in New Zealand. The use of the term 'wood farms' is deliberate, as *Pinus radiata* is grown in a way that is designed to optimise the timber yield, which is not necessarily what is best for the holistic and ecological health of the forest.

Once the lumber has been grown and harvested in New Zealand, it is shipped to the Netherlands, where the 'engineering' takes place. The newly harvested pine is 'pickled' using acetic anhydride, which is a waste product from the photographic film business. Acetic anhydride is sometimes described as a really strong vinegar, but is in fact a man-made chemical that comes from a refinery. When radiata pine is 'pickled' in acetic anhydride, it alters the cell structure of the wood. According to Accsys, the owner of Accoya:

The process alters the cell structure of wood, improving its technical properties and making it much stronger and more durable. Unmodified wood contains 'free hydroxyl groups' that absorb and release water as weather conditions change. This makes standard wood susceptible to expansion and contraction.[41]

Once again, just like the period right after World War II, chemical waste products are being utilised in order to create a solution to a non-existent problem. The starting point here is not to work with the twin realities of wood and weather, but to try to control them. We have seen the untold damage this mindset has had in the past, so I believe some caution about this new so-called 'miracle wood'[42] is in order.

Though the radiata pine is grown in New Zealand, the pickling is done in the Netherlands. Add to this the fact that the acetic anhydride is mainly manufactured by a firm in Wisconsin, USA, and we are left with an engineered timber with a huge carbon footprint. By the time that Accoya hits the shelves of a builder's merchant in Europe, it has travelled at least 27,000–30,000km (17,000–19,000 miles), the distance from Auckland to Rotterdam. For it to make it to sale in the USA, the distance is more like 31,500–35,000km (19,500–22,000 miles).[43] Surely this fact alone – never mind the shipping miles of the acetic anhydride – completely disqualifies Accoya as a

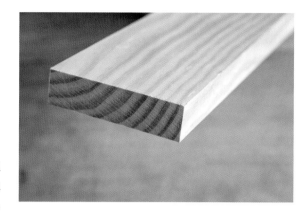

Cross-section of Accoya.

building material that should be seriously considered. Shipping timber halfway across the planet is simply not necessary, when excellent options are already available locally. Shipping Accoya to northern Europe or the US Pacific coast seems rather like the idea of shipping snow to Antarctica.

Accoya is undoubtedly preferable to the use of exotic hardwoods that have been unsustainably harvested in jungles and rainforests. The appeal of engineered wood is likely to be particularly great to those using plastic paint systems, as this type of 'timber' is more stable, which makes it less likely to form hairline cracks that could let water in. However, using linseed paint would make this concern a moot point and there is plenty of indigenous timber available with a fraction of the embodied energy.

## Chapter Six

# Tools and Accompaniments

Linseed paint is a relatively simple product with a straightforward application process. However, getting the best from it relies on using the right tools and accompaniments for the job.

## WHAT WILL YOU NEED FOR A PROJECT USING LINSEED OIL PAINT?

For best results, I would recommend gathering the following supplies before you get started with your project:

- the linseed paint itself
- oil to dilute the paint for a primer coat
- a measuring jug and container to mix the primer coat
- something to mix the paint with
- rags to wipe brushes and clean up any drips
- good-quality brushes
- hand soap and/or brown soap for cleaning brushes
- sandpaper for wooden surfaces/wire brush for metal surfaces.

Depending on the nature of the project, the desired finish and if any repairs are needed to the surface, you may also require:

- shellac
- linseed putty
- oakum
- linseed varnish.

Supplies needed for your linseed oil project.

## BRUSHES

Paintbrushes come in all shapes and sizes. However, the most important consideration here is choosing a brush with the right type of bristle. Linseed paint should always be applied in thin coats, ideally with an even finish and minimal visible brushstrokes. In order to achieve this, it is well worth investing in decent quality brushes.

Paintbrushes consist of four parts: the filament; the stock; the ferrule; and the handle. The more expensive the brush, the better quality these components should be. The better the quality of the brush, the stronger the hold it will have of the bristles. This is important, as paintbrushes that regularly shed bristles can result in a poor finish.

## Why natural bristles are best

Densely filled natural bristles made of ox or hog hair are widely considered to be best for use with linseed paint. Synthetic brushes simply tend not to give a smooth enough finish. Not only does this compromise the finished look of the paint, it also makes the job of applying it far harder than it needs to be.

The reason for this is, once again, all down to the science of surface tension. Linseed oil has a far lower surface tension than water, which adheres perfectly to the slightly scaly surface of natural bristle. Synthetic bristle, in comparison, are too smooth and the paint will not adhere to them as well. This can result in the paint 'dragging' during application.

Not all natural bristles will perform as well as others. There is a significant difference in hog hair from animals that have been reared for food versus those that have not, and those that have been reared in warmer climates versus those reared in colder ones. The variety of hog bristles that is best for paintbrushes usually come from China and India.

It is also worth keeping in mind that natural bristles will shape to the way you hold the brush, a bit like a fountain pen adapts to the writer. This will mean that the more you use a brush, the easier and smoother it will be. It is possible to purchase hybrid brushes that contain both natural and synthetic bristles, but generally these do not work nearly as well as the real thing.

## Which shape of brushes do you need?

There are all sorts of different shapes of brushes available. Often, the type of shape you choose is down to personal preference – for example, which shape do you feel gives you the best control? To start with, it might be wise to choose a brush in a size smaller than you usually would, as dense natural brushes will likely hold more linseed paint than you expect. However, a complete set of brushes should include a loading brush, a detail brush and a laying-off brush.

### Loading brush

A loading brush is used to get the paint out of the tin and on to the surface. Some people like to use a round brush for this, but I find that oval works just as well. You may wish to vary the size of the brush depending on the project; a larger brush might be easier if you're painting a large or rough surface.

### Detail brush

For delicate or detail work such as painting glazing bars, working in rebates or getting into corners and

Used brush collection.

Loading of a brush.

Sash brush.                              Laying-off brush.

there is not really any such thing as a 'budget' natural brush, good-quality natural brushes will last for years and will no doubt work out as much better value over time.

There are several manufacturers of good-quality natural brushes. My favourites are Guldberg, based in Denmark, and Gnesta, based in Sweden. I would describe Gnesta as the Rolls-Royce of brushes. They really do give an excellent finish. For a professional, or someone with a big project on their hands, these brushes are likely to be a worthy investment, especially considering that they only get better over time. Guldberg brushes are a little cheaper, but are still of excellent quality.

edges, you will want to use a brush that gives a great deal of control. For these sorts of jobs, I like to use a sash brush, which is a round brush with the tip of the bristles cut into a point.

## Laying-off brush

Laying off is a step that helps to give an excellent finish. It can be done at the end of every coat if you wish, but is absolutely essential for the final coat. You will need a soft laying-off brush to go over the paint you have just applied. Use long, gentle, sweeping strokes in the direction of the grain. This will help to level out the paint and remove any visible brushstrokes.

## Where to buy brushes

Synthetic brushes can now be bought so cheaply that there is a tendency to view them as a disposable product. Many people pick up a new pack of brushes along with each tin of paint, then throw them away when the job is done. Not only is this an unnecessary drain on resources, it is also a practice that's likely to add up quickly. Though it is true that

## Cleaning and caring for your brushes

Once you have invested in good-quality brushes, it makes sense to look after them properly. Do not let your brushes dry out with paint on them. They can be cleaned by rubbing them with a little brown soap and running them under lukewarm water. It is important to get all the paint out, but also to rinse out all the soap residue. Any residual soap left on the brush could interfere with the paint for your next project. Once your brushes have been fully rinsed, hang them to dry.

Brush cleaning with brown soap.

*The lazier option*

It does not always make sense to spend time cleaning out every last bit of paint and soap from a brush, especially if you are stopping part way through a project. If you want to protect your brushes while you stop for a tea break or overnight, you can take the easy way out and suspend the brushes in some raw linseed oil. To do this, brush off excess paint on a piece of cardboard or timber, then pop the brushes in a plastic cup or old jam jar filled with raw linseed oil. As long as the bristles are completely submerged, your brushes will be fine until you're ready to continue your project.

If you're planning to store your brushes in this way for the longer term, make sure that the jars are out of direct sunlight and change the oil after every couple of jobs. I also recommend keeping a jar for each colour group, or at least separating dark and light colours, to avoid possible cross-contamination.

## OTHER ACCOMPANIMENTS

### Balsam turpentine

I prefer the name 'balsam turpentine', but this product is also sometimes referred to as 'gum turpentine' and, occasionally, 'spirit of turpentine' or 'wood turpentine'. Balsam turpentine is a clear, low-viscosity essential oil. It is extracted from the resin overflow (balsam) of various species of pine, via a process of steam distillation. It is worth mentioning here that 'gum' is a colloquial name for tree resin, hence the alternative title of 'gum turpentine'.

Each bottle of balsam turpentine smells like it contains a whole pine forest. As a rule, it will consist of around 70 per cent rosin resin and 30 per cent turpentine oil. The world's pine forests release several million tonnes of turpentine oil into the atmosphere every year. This is nothing new; it has been happening for millions of years and does not damage the atmosphere. Balsam turpentine is the world's most produced essential oil, with about half of it coming from the USA. Argentina and Brazil are also major producers, followed by Scandinavia, China, Portugal, Spain and the Baltic states.

*How is balsam turpentine used with linseed paint?*

Balsam turpentine has one important use with linseed paint – as a mixer to create a primer coat. If you are painting untreated timber (either new or stripped down), I always recommend starting with a primer coat. This should consist of 50 per cent linseed paint, 35 per cent raw linseed oil and 15 per cent balsam turpentine. The balsam turpentine is a vital part of this mixture for two reasons:

Brushes sitting in oil.

Bottle of balsam turpentine.

- to balance out the increased drying time caused by adding raw linseed oil
- to cut through any resins that may still be present in the timber.

*Is balsam turpentine the same as turps?*

On hearing the name balsam turpentine, many people will confuse this natural essential oil with petrochemical versions of turps, such as white spirit or mineral turpentine. As *Ullmann's Encyclopedia of Industrial Chemistry* (first published in 1914) points out, these petrochemical versions have a very different chemical constituency.[44] They therefore should not be used in the same way.

White spirit or any other off the shelf turps from your local builders' merchant is not suitable for use with linseed paint. It should not be used to thin linseed paint, as part of a primer coat, or even to clean brushes used with linseed paint.

## Shellac

Shellac is an effective stain and resin blocker, derived from the hypoallergenic resin secreted by the female lac bug. The lac bug secretes the shellac to create a cocoon, which leaves a coating on the trees in forests in India and Thailand. This shellac is harvested in flakes, which are then mixed with denatured alcohol.

Though aluminium primers are more effective for blocking resin, when shellac is applied in two coats it is usually highly efficient. Like aluminium primers, the overlapping flakes that make up shellac form an impervious barrier that seals in and stops resin being pushed out from any knots in the wood.

When using shellac knotting primer, it should be applied in two thin coats. You will not be able to achieve a good finish if shellac is applied too thickly, as it will be visible through the final layers of paint. Shellac can also wrinkle if it is applied too thickly.

Shellac flakes.

Shellac dissolved in alcohol.

## Linseed soap

Linseed soap is made by boiling linseed oil with lye. This process creates an excellent, all-round cleaning soap, which is as nourishing as it is effective. It is equally good for cleaning timber and brushes as it is for cleaning hands.

Linseed soap.

## Chapter Seven

# How to Apply Linseed Paint on Timber

Timber is the traditional surface on which to apply linseed paint. It is most commonly used for exterior timber projects such as windows, doors, balustrades, decking, fencing and sheds. If you are embarking on such a project – or indeed on any other kind of timber project – you may be relieved to know that working with linseed paint really isn't rocket science. However, it is a bit different from working with conventional plastic paint, so in this chapter you will find clear, step-by-step instructions for achieving the best possible results.

## SCOPING THE PROJECT AND ASSESSING REQUIREMENTS

Everything starts with understanding your project. The first task of any painting project should be to inspect the timber closely and assess whether any repairs are needed. Make sure that you take extra time when checking horizontal surfaces on the lower third of the structure, as these areas are the most vulnerable and the most likely to have suffered damage.

Do keep in mind that some kinds of damage may not be obvious at first glance, especially if the timber has been previously painted. Plastic paint can cover up all manner of issues, so you may need to strip back the timber before you can make a full assessment. This may be particularly crucial if you are repainting wooden window casings. It is likely to be well worth scraping paint off the sills and lower glazing bars to get a full idea of the condition of the wood.

## Gathering your tools

Preparing all your tools in advance can save time and ensure that your project runs more smoothly. Before you open the tin of paint to begin, you may want to make sure that you have the following close to hand:

- sander/sandpaper/hot-air gun/infrared gun (for removal of previous paint)
- shellac knotting primer
- oakum and linseed putty (in case repairs are needed)
- linseed paint in the colour of your choice
- raw linseed oil
- balsam or pine turpentine (make sure this is natural turpentine, not white spirit)
- empty tin or container (for mixing a primer coat in)
- stirring stick
- good-quality paintbrushes
- rags for any necessary clean-ups (remember to submerge any rags that have come into contact with linseed oil or paint in water before throwing them away)
- clean piece of cardboard or timber
- brown soap or plastic cup filled with 4cm (1.5in) of raw linseed oil.

## PREPARING THE SURFACE

Linseed paint can only perform as well as the surface or substrate on which it is painted. Though you can certainly choose to paint over plastic paint with linseed paint, it will only be able to perform as well as the existing paint. This means that the existing paint will continue to trap moisture inside the timber and may well continue to flake or peel, taking the linseed paint with it when it does.

The prospect of needing to remove existing paint can be daunting. It is a very time-consuming step, which can be tedious if doing it yourself, or expensive if paying a professional to do it on your behalf. However, it really is an essential part of the process if you want to get the full benefit of linseed paint and prolong the lifespan of both the paint job and the timber itself.

When linseed paint is applied to bare timber (whether to new timber, or timber that has been properly stripped down), this is where it can really shine. If the linseed paint is applied properly to a bare timber surface, it will not flake or peel. Indeed, depending on the circumstances, it may not ever need to be painted again. Even if it does need an occasional extra coat of paint over the decades to come, the linseed paint will not need to be removed or sanded down. In other words, taking the time now to strip back the timber properly will likely save many hours of sanding, repainting and refinishing in the future.

Testing for plastic paint with denatured alcohol.

## Checking whether paint needs removing

As mentioned above, only plastic paints, that is, latex, acrylic and alkyd-based paints, need removing. If you are not sure whether you are dealing with a modern plastic paint, there is an easy way to check. Using a cotton swab, rub some denatured alcohol on the surface. Plastic paints will dissolve, whereas linseed paint or lime wash will not. The images here are from a test patch at Wilton House Museum in Richmond, VA. It was always believed that the blue colour was one of the original paint layers. However, a quick test showed that this was not the case and it was, in fact, a relatively modern coat of plastic paint.

Testing for plastic paint, showing how it comes off easily.

## How to remove paint

The traditional way to remove paint is with a sander and good, old-fashioned elbow grease. However, this can be a tedious and time-consuming job, so if you have a lot of paint to remove you may want to consider ways to speed things up, such as using a hot-air gun, or an infrared gun.

### Checking for lead pigments

Before you get stuck into paint removal, it is important to consider the age of the paint and the possibility that it might contain lead pigments. Many paint manufacturers stopped using lead pigments in the 1960s, though quantities of lead were still used in primers and certain specialist paints until it was banned in 1992. If you are removing paint from wood that predates this, such as from skirting boards or window frames in a 1930s or 1950s property, it's likely that some of the older layers of paint will contain lead.

If in doubt, it is a good idea to do a test for the presence of lead. There are many inexpensive test kits available that just require a quick swab of the paint. They will usually give a result in less than a minute. Lead testing kits work using the compound sodium rhodizonate, which turns red when it comes into contact with lead. The swab itself will contain the compound, so once you have run it over the paint in question, you should be able to see quickly and easily if any lead is present.

If the paint you are hoping to strip does contain lead, you should *not* attempt to sand it. Sanding creates a lot of dust and when lead is present, this dust will contain harmful particles that could result in lead poisoning. In these cases, the only options for removing the paint will be using a chemical peel or an infrared gun. Even after its safe removal, you will still be working with a surface that has had lead paint on it, so you will need to take extra precautions, such as wearing gloves and a mask and washing your hands regularly. The CLAW (Control

of Lead at Work) Regulations 2002 (UK) set out the best practice methods for managing the removal of lead paint.

If you have found lead paint on a surface you are working on, it may be tempting just to paint over it. Though this may seem like a safer and more efficient

Lead test – wetting the tip.

Swabbing the surface.

If the tip goes red, the paint contains lead.

option, it is simply likely to prolong the problem, as the lead paint will almost certainly cause the top layer of paint to flake.

## Chemical peels

Chemical peels can certainly remove paint with far less effort than other options. Despite this, they are not always the best choice. For one thing, the manufacturing process used to create them has a high carbon footprint, so they are not an environmentally friendly option, especially if you are trying to reduce your plastic use.

There is also a high risk that the chemical peel will leave behind chemical residue on the wood, which could react with the new paint. The likelihood of this can be reduced by ensuring that you always neutralise the timber after a chemical peel has been applied, but it does not remove the risk altogether. However, in cases where lead paint is present, or the wood contains very fine detailed work or filigree, a chemical peel might be the only practical solution.

## Hot-air guns

Hot-air guns can be an efficient way to remove paint from a surface. They work by using convection heat at around 250–750°C (480–1,380°F) to heat the paint and allow it to be easily scraped away. A hot-air gun should be held at around a 45-degree angle from the surface and not kept in one place for too long, otherwise it may burn the paint.

However, a hot-air gun is not suitable if lead is present in the paint. This is because when lead particles are heated to above 400°C (750°F), they can release toxic fumes. As hot-air guns often get hotter than this, it just isn't worth the risk. Hot-air guns can also be problematic if you are using them to strip paint off a surface with glass nearby, such as a window frame. No matter how careful you are, the heat from the gun can often cause glass to crack.

## Infrared heaters

One of the best methods for removing paint is by using an infrared heater. The leading brand is called Speedheater and was invented in Sweden by Birger Ericson. Unlike a hot-air gun, infrared heaters don't just heat everything. Instead, they use a wavelength that activates the water molecules in the paint to be removed. Once activated, these water molecules bubble up, which makes it easy to scrape off the paint. Of course, this only removes paint that traps water molecules, such as plastic or petrochemical paints. Any older layers of linseed paint will be left undamaged, which can then be painted straight over with a fresh coat of linseed paint. (If this happens, you will often find that the old linseed paint will act as a perfect primer coat.)

Not only does an infrared gun work in a more targeted way than a hot-air gun, it is also cooler. When in use, the temperature will stay between 100 and 160°C (210–320°F). This makes it highly unlikely to cause any scorched wood, nor to crack any adjacent panes of glass (the heat is generated by radiation rather than by convection). The lower temperature of the infrared gun is also great news for removing paint that contains lead pigments. Lead does not let off toxic fumes until it is heated to around 400°C (750°F), which is far hotter than an infrared gun.

The IVF Industrial Research and Development Institute in Mölndal tested the Speedheater infrared

Infrared paint remover in action.

guns in 2005/06 to determine their safety for removing lead paint. They found that the monitored lead exposure during the removal of lead-pigmented paint 'ranged from 0.5 to 5.1µg/m$^3$, well below permissible exposure limit'.[45] This is particularly encouraging, considering that the tests were carried out on real-world projects rather than in a lab setting. This means that even under worst-case conditions, the Speedheater released less than 10 per cent of the legally accepted threshold of lead limits, as per both Swedish and American regulations. The Speedheater can therefore be used to remove lead paint safely; in fact, in the USA it is the only legally approved method.

Though infrared speed guns do not create any dust when the paint bubbles up to be scraped away, care should be taken over any removed scraps of paint once they begin to dry out. To avoid any dust being created by paint scraps building up on the floor around a project, ensure that these are cleared up frequently and safely disposed of. Protective clothing should be worn throughout the process and always follow the manufacturer's instructions.

## Precautions for new timber

If you are using new timber, you won't have the laborious task of removing any previous layers of paint. However, it is important to do some research into how the new wood is supplied.

Many joinery companies or DIY shops will supply wooden objects such as window frames, fence panels or sheds pre-treated. (This is sometimes called 'factory sprayed'.) Though this is generally sold as a good thing, it is not necessarily the case if you are planning on painting the wood with linseed paint. These kinds of wood treatments make it much harder for the linseed oil and pigments to be fully absorbed into the timber, which can greatly reduce the lifespan of the paint job. If you have the luxury of choice when using new timber, the best option for these purposes is likely to be untreated Douglas fir.

## Precautions for hardwoods

If you are preparing a hardwood such as teak, cedar or oak for painting, you may need to add a few extra steps. Some types of hardwood can be much oilier than softwoods, which can prevent paint from adhering and drying properly. This can be avoided by washing the surface thoroughly with a solvent or acetone before painting. The best results are usually achieved with a stiff scrubbing brush. Once you have finished this, be sure to allow plenty of time for the surface to dry and for the acetone or solvent to evaporate completely.

## Making wood repairs

Wood repairs can be sorted into three broad categories:

- small repairs
- medium repairs
- large and structural repairs.

The best technique to use will vary depending on the category of repair, but for a successful result you should choose natural materials and traditional methods. The recommended products are linseed putty, oakum and timber.

### Small repairs

For small repairs, start by establishing whether the repair is actually necessary. It's very common for surface erosion to cause small rills in the surface of timber. This is often seen on gates and siding. However, this type of rill does not tend to cause any issues in the wood or affect its strength. They are also notoriously difficult to fill or smooth out, as there is very little for putty or other fillers to cling to, so the filler often falls out over time, which looks even messier.

If you are dealing with this kind of rill, it's usually better to leave it as it is. Yes, the timber may no longer look perfectly uniform, but it is not really

Rills in timber.

Filling a hole with oakum.

'damaged'. Don't be tempted to address the problem by using a thicker layer of linseed paint in eroded areas. There is no benefit to doing this, as all that will happen is that the thicker paint will never fully dry out and cure.

Small repairs will be needed in the case of holes left behind by drills, nails, screws or similar. In these cases, a small amount of linseed putty can be used to fill the hole. Once this has dried, it can then be sanded smooth and painted along with the rest of the surface. If the holes are very small, there may not be sufficient surface area for linseed putty to adhere to. A good way round this is to make the hole big enough to work with. Drilling the hole with a 6–7mm drill bit is usually sufficient.

Filling a hole with putty on oakum.

## Medium repairs

Medium repairs are anything more than 2–5cm (1–2in). Holes on the smaller size of this scale can still be filled by using linseed putty. However, more substantial holes from 5cm (2in) should not be filled with just linseed putty, as it will not be strong enough alone. Instead, you will need to pack the hole with oakum first and then fill the gaps with linseed putty. Make sure to leave around 1cm (0.4in) between the oakum and the surface of the timber, then fill this space with linseed putty.

## Large and structural repairs

If you are dealing with a large hole or a structural section such as a corner or a joint, you will likely need to repair it by splicing in a piece of timber. There are some notes on the process of doing this below, but it is wise to get advice from a trusted joiner before you begin.

You will want to use stripped, untreated timber for this. A section of salvaged timber would be preferable, but high-quality Douglas fir will work well if new is the only option.

1. Cut the new/salvaged section of timber to the right size.
2. Use wood glue to secure it into place.

3. Sand down the whole surface.
4. Paint the entire surface as one. There should not be any noticeable difference in the absorption of the linseed paint between the existing and repaired parts of the timber.

## Final steps

Following are the final steps in preparing a surface for painting:

1. Sand down the surface using 100–120 grit sandpaper. (This step is important even with timber that has never been painted before, as it will

Spliced-in wood repair.

Sanding the surface.

Wiping the surface.

Applying shellac.

make it easier for the linseed paint to adhere to the surface.)

2. Once you have finished sanding, wipe the surface with a wet, lint-free rag (an old T-shirt or tea towel is ideal). Then, leave the surface to dry completely.

3. Apply a coat of shellac knotting primer to any knots. You can use a cheap brush for this. Leave the coat to dry (which should take about an hour), then apply a second coat and leave to dry.

4. The surface is now ready for painting.

## APPLYING THE PAINT

The following steps have been designed to achieve the best possible finish on wooden surfaces such as doors, window frames and trims.

1. Open the tin of paint and check whether it has formed a skin. This is completely normal (it just means that some oxygen has got in) and does not affect the rest of the paint. If there is a skin, make sure you scrape it off and discard it; do not stir it into the paint.

    If it is difficult to remove the skin, the best option will be to strain the paint. Fortunately, this can be done very easily, by using an old pair of nylon tights or stockings. Tie the tights/stockings over the top of an empty paint tin, then pour the paint that needs to be strained into this tin, through the tights. The nylon will filter out anything that should not be there.

2. Stir the paint thoroughly to ensure that no pigments are stuck at the bottom of the tin. Ideally, spend about five minutes doing this.

3. Mix your primer coat. This should be approximately 50 per cent paint, 35 per cent raw linseed oil and 15 per cent balsam turpentine (note that this can *not* be substituted with white spirit or turps). An easy way to measure these quantities is by marking 5cm (2in), 3.5cm (1.5in) and 1.5cm (0.5in) on a stirring stick or a transparent measuring cup. Don't worry if your ratios aren't completely accurate with these quantities. They are simply an indication and nothing will go wrong if they're slightly out.

    If you are painting a hardwood surface, you will want to add a solvent to the primer coat. This should make up about 10 per cent of the total volume.

4. Stir the primer mix well, then put a small amount on a good-quality, natural bristle brush. Apply in a thin coat, working in cross-sections. Make sure to stir the primer mix regularly.

This image shows a typical example of skin forming on the paint. This is completely normal and happens when air gets to it.

The best way to deal with this is by scraping off the skin. Do not stir it into the paint.

Once you have loosened the edges of the skin, scoop it out. Then stir the rest of the paint and you can start using it.

If skin or other bits have inadvertently got into the paint, you might have to strain it. Use an old stocking to act as a sieve, as shown in the picture.

Once the stocking is in place, carefully pour the paint, making sure the stocking stays attached in place.

The paint will take a few seconds to run through, and the stocking will capture any particles that are too large.

Once the paint has run through, carefully remove the stocking and discard.

Unstirred paint.

Stirred paint.

Marking the stirring stick.

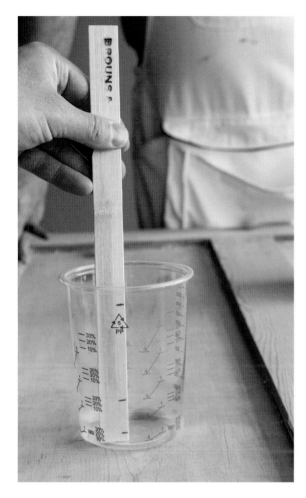

Measuring stick in a cup.

2. Pour 35 per cent raw linseed oil.

3. Pour 15 per cent balsam turpentine.

1. Pour 50 per cent paint in an empty cup.

5. When you have achieved full coverage, finish the coat with long, even strokes in the direction of the grain.

6. Leave the coat to dry completely. If you are painting outside in spring, summer or early autumn with reasonably good weather, this should only take twenty-four hours. A good first coat will usually look patchy, especially if you have used a shellac knotting primer. This patchiness is generally caused by varying absorption levels; areas where the timber has more fully absorbed the paint will look darker. Don't worry, this will even out with subsequent coats.

Applying the paint in cross-sections.

Laying-off.

Patchy look after the first coat.

7. Before starting the second coat, give the fully dry first coat a light key with 200 grit sandpaper.

8. The second coat should be painted straight from the tin – there is no need to dilute it this time. Make sure that you give the tin a really good mix first and continue to paint in thin coats.

9. Once the second coat is finished, again you will need to leave it until it is completely dry. This is likely to take longer than the primer coat. In ideal weather conditions, expect to leave the coat for between twenty-four and forty-eight hours.

10. Once the second coat has dried, it should have a mid-sheen finish that is less patchy than the primer coat. Give it a light key with 200 grit sandpaper before starting the third coat.

11. Apply the third and final coat straight from the tin, using thin, even strokes.

12. Once full coverage for the coat has been achieved, you will need to lay off the paint to make sure that it is well distributed, with no visible brushstrokes. With a soft laying-off brush, make long, gentle sweeping strokes in the direction of the grain.

13. Leave the coat to dry completely. Again, this is likely to take between twenty-four and forty-eight hours; longer if weather conditions are not ideal. Once the third coat dries, it should produce a glossy finish.

Sanding after the primer coat.

Applying the final coat.

Applying the second coat straight from the tin.

Sanding the second coat.

Laying off the final coat.

## CLEANING UP AND STORING PAINT

1. When stopping mid-project, such as between coats, use a lint-free rag or clean cardboard to wipe any excess paint off each brush. The brushes can then be placed in a beaker containing a few centimetres of raw linseed oil, ensuring that the bristles are fully covered.

2. If you have finished a project and are ready to put your brushes away properly, wipe off any excess paint with a rag, then use brown soap and warm water to rinse the brushes completely. Make sure that no soap is left in the bristles, as this could compromise future painting projects. Hang the brushes to dry.

3. Any rags that you have used should be soaked in water before they are thrown away. Alternatively, they can be left in direct sunlight to dry out completely. Rags soaked in linseed paint or linseed oil should never be left unattended, as it is possible for them to self-ignite.

Cleaning the brush with linseed soap.

The best way to avoid a skin forming is by putting some cling film on the surface of the paint.

Brushing out excess paint.

Make sure to press the cling film on top of the paint and up against the inside wall of the tin so no air can get to it.

4. When putting paint away, ensure that you close the lid tightly. This prevents oxygen from getting into the tin and forming a skin. If the lid will no longer form a tight seal, you can use cling film to protect the paint. Cover the surface of the paint and the inside wall of the tin with the cling film, then put the lid on top.
5. Paint tins should be stored out of direct sunlight and turned every so often.

## SPECIALIST APPLICATIONS

### Painting rough, unplaned timber

Surface preparation may be unnecessary when painting unplaned timber, such as a fence or a shed. In these cases, you will not need to do any prep beyond removing any existing paint. You do not need to sand the surface, nor treat any knots with shellac knotting primer.

The painting process is also likely to be different because you will hopefully only need to do one coat. Because surfaces like these do not get any mechanical wear, the number of coats you need to put on is down to aesthetics more than anything else. You can apply paint straight from the tin; no primer coat is needed. Load the brush with more paint than you would when working on a smooth timber surface

Painting rough-sawn timber in one coat.

and take your time to really work the paint into the timber using cross-strokes and circular motions. If you're taking on a project like this, be prepared for some hard, physical work. However, you can do so safely in the knowledge that you will not have to repaint any time soon.

### Painting window frames with double glazing

Linseed paint works brilliantly on window frames and is very commonly used for this purpose. However, some caution is required when using linseed paint alongside double-glazing seals. This is particularly important when using double-glazing systems designed for use in historical windows, such as Histoglass. These units are carefully sealed in order to keep the gas in the units and any moisture out. The complicating factor here is that these seals are usually made of polyurethane or polysulphide, neither of which should come into direct contact with linseed oil. Fortunately, there is a simple workaround:

1. Prime the window rebates with two coats of shellac knotting primer, making sure to let both coats dry fully.
2. When the shellac knotting primer is completely dry, install the glazing panes with a silicone or siloxane resin-based bedding compound.

Rough-sawn timber.

# Using Linseed Paint when installing (thin) double glazing

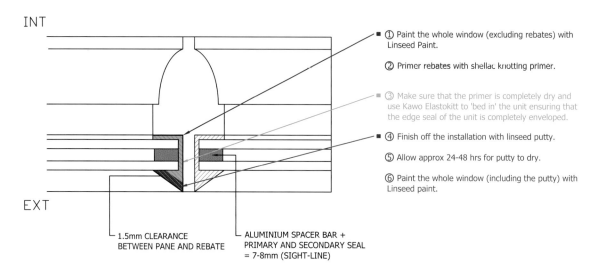

INT

① Paint the whole window (excluding rebates) with Linseed Paint.

② Primer rebates with shellac knotting primer.

③ Make sure that the primer is completely dry and use Kawo Elastokitt to 'bed in' the unit ensuring that the edge seal of the unit is completely enveloped.

④ Finish off the installation with linseed putty.

⑤ Allow approx 24-48 hrs for putty to dry.

⑥ Paint the whole window (including the putty) with Linseed paint.

EXT

1.5mm CLEARANCE BETWEEN PANE AND REBATE

ALUMINIUM SPACER BAR + PRIMARY AND SECONDARY SEAL = 7-8mm (SIGHT-LINE)

Sketch of linseed paint in combination with thin double-glazing.

(KAWO Elastokitt is one of the best on the market.) This bedding compound will create a U-shaped profile, which will envelope the edge seal of the unit.

3. The installation can then be finished on the outer face using either a timber bead or linseed putty.

4. Once everything else has dried, the whole window frame can be painted using linseed paint. Follow the general application instructions for this.

## WHAT TO AVOID

### Saturating timber with linseed oil

You may have come across advice to paint a primer coat consisting of either raw or boiled linseed oil. This is absolutely not necessary and, in fact, is best avoided.

One of the main reasons that linseed paint works so well is due to the combination of oil and pigments. If timber is covered with raw or boiled linseed oil before it is painted, the timber will already be saturated when you come to paint it with linseed paint, meaning that the oil that contains pigments will not be able to penetrate the timber. When pigments can only lie on the surface of the timber, they will not be able to provide such long-lasting protection from the elements.

### Heating linseed oil or paint

There have also been instances where people have been advised to use heated raw linseed oil as a primer. This is usually carried out with by using a heating element in a large dipping tank filled with linseed oil. The reason given for doing this is typically that heating raw linseed oil will make it even thinner, meaning that it is better able to penetrate timber.

However, this completely ignores some very basic rules of physics. When hot oil is used to penetrate timber, it will not stay hot forever. When the oil cools to room temperature, it will naturally begin to expand, which then runs the risk of warping and cracking the timber from within. (The easiest way to understand how this process works is by considering the difference in volume between water and ice.) This is a particular issue when the timber components of something like a gate have been soaked separately, as afterwards they may not fit together again properly.

## Chapter Eight

# Applying Linseed Paint on Metal

Linseed paint is an excellent choice for painting metal. Not only does it adhere really well to these sorts of surfaces, it is also an effective way to protect metal from rust and corrosion. If you are planning to use linseed paint on metal, following the steps outlined Linseed paint is an excellent choice for painting metal. Not only does it adhere really well to these sorts of surfaces, it is also an effective way to protect metal from rust and corrosion. If you are planning to use linseed paint on metal, following the steps outlined in this chapter will help you to achieve the best possible results.

## SCOPING THE PROJECT AND ASSESSING REQUIREMENTS

Half of the success of a paint job is determined before you have even picked up a brush. It is important to take the time to assess the surface fully before starting to paint. This is particularly important when working on a restoration or preservation project.

Check for weak points in the metal and particularly any places where rust has appeared. In many cases, rust will be superficial and you will be able to remove it with a steel wire brush. If there are any places where rust has worn through the metal, this will need to be repaired. Unlike with wood, metal repairs usually need to be carried out by a professional metal worker.

### Gathering your tools

Making an inventory of what you will need through-out a project and ensuring that they are all to hand before you begin can save much time and frustration later on. If you are planning a project with linseed paint and a metal surface, you will likely need:

- iron-oxide primer
- linseed paint in the colour of your choice
- balsam or pine turpentine (make sure this is natural turpentine, not white spirit)
- empty tin or container (for mixing the primer coat in)
- stirring stick
- good-quality paintbrushes
- rags for any necessary clean-ups (remember to submerge any rags that have come into contact with linseed oil or paint in water before throwing them away)
- clean piece of cardboard or timber
- brown soap or a plastic cup filled with 4cm (1.5in) of raw linseed oil.

### A note on iron-oxide primer

There is a specialist linseed paint primer designed to be used on metal. It is often known as 'armour paint' because of the structure of its main ingredients: iron haematite oxide or aluminium. These ingredients work with the low surface tension of linseed oil to ensure that water cannot penetrate the paint to reach the metal.

When you look at a metal surface or run your hand along it, it will seem perfectly smooth. In fact, at a microscopic level, this is not the case. Rather, a metal surface will have lots of peaks and troughs that can fill with water molecules and begin to oxidise over time. When a primer coat bonds to a metal surface, it will fill these crevices so that water can't.

## PREPARING THE SURFACE

Though there are clear differences in technique when painting a metal surface versus a wooden one, the basic premise is the same. The better the surface is prepared before starting, the better the paint will adhere to it and protect whatever is underneath. For best results, it is important to remove any existing paint on the surface. This can be fiddly and time-consuming, but time invested at this stage will be time saved in terms of maintenance further down the line.

When preparing a metal surface for linseed paint, it is important to keep in mind just how quickly metal can rust. You will need to be particularly aware of this if you are working on an exterior project and there is a high humidity level.

If you are removing an earlier layer of paint in order to repaint with linseed oil, you will not want to leave the bare metal underneath exposed for any longer than is necessary. Ideally, a primer coat should be applied almost as soon as the existing paint has been removed. It is best to work your way along in small sections. Remove any existing paint in each section, then prepare the surface underneath and paint on the primer *before* moving to the next section.

### How to remove paint from metal

Just like when removing paint from wood, the traditional way to remove paint from metal is with a sander and good, old-fashioned elbow grease. However, this can be a tedious and time-consuming job, so if you have a lot of paint to remove you may want to consider ways to speed things up, such as using a hot-air gun, or an infrared gun.

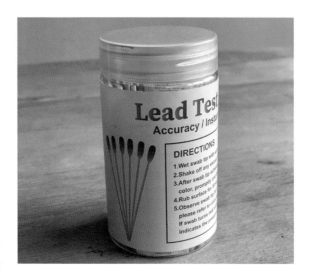

Lead testing kit.

*Checking for lead pigments*

Before you get stuck into paint removal, it is important to consider the age of the paint you are removing and the possibility that it might contain lead pigments. Many paint manufacturers stopped using lead pigments in the 1960s, though quantities of lead were still used in primers and specialist paints until it was banned in 1992. If you are removing paint from metal that predates this, such as from metal railings around a Victorian property, it is likely that some of the older layers of paint will contain lead.

If in doubt, it is a good idea to do a test for the presence of lead. There are many inexpensive test kits available that just require a quick swab of the paint. They will usually give you a result in less than a minute. Lead testing kits work using the compound sodium rhodizonate, which turns red when it comes in contact with lead. The swab itself will contain the compound, so once you have run it over the paint in question, you should be able to see quickly and easily if any lead is present.

If the paint you are hoping to strip does contain lead, you should *not* attempt to sand it. Sanding creates a lot of dust and when lead is present in the paint, this dust will contain harmful particles that could lead to lead poisoning. In these cases, the only options for removing the paint will be using a chemical peel or an infrared gun.

## Chemical peels

Chemical peels can certainly remove paint with far less effort than other options. Despite this, they are not always the best option. For one thing, the manufacturing process used to create them has a high carbon footprint, so they are not a very environmentally friendly option, especially if you are trying to reduce your plastic use.

There is also a high risk that the chemical peel will leave behind chemical residue on the surface of the metal, which could react with the new paint. The likelihood of this can be reduced by ensuring that you always neutralise the surface after a chemical peel has been applied, but it does not remove the risk altogether. Despite this, in cases where lead paint is present, or the metal contains very fine detailed work, a chemical peel might be the only practical solution.

## Hot-air guns

Hot-air guns can be an efficient way to remove paint from a surface. They work by using convection heat at around 250–750°C (480–1,380°F) to heat the paint and allow it to be easily scraped away. A hot air gun should be held at around a 45-degree angle from the surface and not kept in one place for too long, otherwise it may burn the paint.

However, a hot air gun is not suitable if lead is present in the paint. This is because when lead particles are heated to above 400°C (750°F), they can release toxic fumes. As hot air guns often get hotter than this, it just isn't worth the risk.

Hot-air guns can also be problematic if you are using them to strip paint off a metal surface with glass nearby. No matter how careful you are, the heat from the gun can often cause glass to crack.

## Infrared heaters

One of the best methods for removing paint is by using an infrared heater. The leading brand is called Speedheater and was invented in Sweden by Birger Ericson. Unlike a hot air gun, infrared heaters don't just heat everything. Instead, they use a wavelength that activates the water molecules in the paint to be removed. Once activated, these water molecules bubble up, which makes it easy to scrape of the paint. Of course, this only removes paint that traps water molecules, such as plastic or petrochemical paints. Any older layers of linseed paint will be left undamaged, which can then be painted straight over with a fresh coat of linseed paint. (If this happens, you will often find that the old linseed paint will act as a perfect primer coat.)

Not only does an infrared gun work in a more targeted way than a hot air gun, it is also cooler. When in use, the temperature will stay between 100 and 160°C (210–320°F). This makes it highly unlikely to cause any scorched paint, nor to crack any adjacent panes of glass (the heat is generated by radiation rather than convection). The lower temperature of the infrared gun is also great news for removing paint that contains lead pigments. Lead doesn't let off toxic fumes until it is heated to around 400°C (750°F), which is far hotter than an infrared gun.

The IVF Industrial Research and Development Institute in Mölndal tested the Speedheater infrared guns in 2005/06 to determine their safety for removing lead paint. They found that the monitored lead exposure during the removal of lead-pigmented paint 'ranged from 0.5 to 5.1μg/m³, well below permissible exposure limit'.[46] This is particularly encouraging, considering that the tests were carried out on real-world projects rather than in a lab setting. This means that even under worst-case conditions, the Speedheader released less than 10 per cent of the legally accepted threshold of lead limits, as per both Swedish and American regulations. The Speedheater can therefore be used to remove lead

Removing rust with a wire brush.

paint safely. In fact, in the USA it is the only legally approved method.

## Final steps

Following are the final steps in preparing a surface for painting:

1. Brush the surface of the metal with a wire brush. (This is important even if the metal is new, as it will aid adhesion and get rid of any oil or wax residue.)
2. 'Wash' the surface with alcohol and a lint-free cloth and dry thoroughly.
3. The surface is now ready to be painted.

## APPLYING THE PAINT

When painting a metal surface, research shows that you will get the best results using a lean to fat approach.[47] Following the steps below will help you to achieve this.

1. Start with a tin of iron-oxide primer. Stir it well for about five minutes, making sure that no pigment is stuck at the bottom of the tin.

2. Mix nine parts iron-oxide primer with one part balsam turpentine (remember, this is *not* the same thing as white spirit or turps). These quantities are an indication; you do not need to worry if your ratios are not exact.
3. Paint on the primer in a very thin coat, making sure to stir the primer and balsam turpentine mix frequently. Once this is done, leave it to dry completely. This should take around eighteen hours in ideal weather conditions.
4. Once the first coat of the iron-oxide primer is dry, it is time to paint a second primer coat. For this second coat, paint the iron-oxide primer straight from the tin. This coat does not need to be diluted with balsam turpentine. Work in cross-sections, then finish in long, even strokes in the direction of any design. Assuming good weather conditions, this coat will need about twenty-four hours to dry.

Stirring the iron-oxide primer.

Pouring the primer paint.

Pouring balsam turpentine into the primer.

Mixing the metal primer thoroughly.

Applying the metal primer in cross-sections.

5. Once the two primer coats are dry to the touch, you can start your finishing coats. Open the paint and check if it has formed a skin. This is completely normal if the paint has been exposed to oxygen. If necessary, scrape the film off and discard it; do not stir it into the paint.

6. Stir the paint thoroughly for about five minutes. Ensure that no pigment is stuck to the bottom of the tin.

7. Apply a thin coat of linseed paint straight from the tin. This coat should dry within twenty-four to forty-eight hours.

8. Apply the final coat.

9. Finishing this final coat, make sure you lay off the paint using a suitable brush. Again, this coat will need between twenty-four to forty-eight hours to dry completely. You should be able to see a real change in the sheen level between coats. This should have changed from a matt sheen for the primer coats to a mid-sheen for the middle coat to a high sheen on the final coat. This is something that only happens with linseed paint.

Iron-oxide metal primer applied.

## CLEANING UP AND STORING PAINT

1. When stopping mid-project, such as between coats, use a lint-free rag or clean cardboard to wipe any excess paint off each brush. The brushes can then be placed in a beaker containing a few centimetres (1 inch) of raw linseed oil, ensuring that the bristles are fully covered.

2. If you have finished a project and are ready to put your brushes away properly, wipe off any excess paint with a rag, then use brown soap and warm water to rinse the brushes completely. Make sure that no soap is left in the bristles, as this could compromise future painting projects. Hang the brushes to dry.

3. Any rags that you have used should be soaked in water before they are thrown away. Alternatively, they can be left in direct sunlight to dry out completely. Rags soaked in linseed paint or linseed oil should never be left unattended, as it is possible for them to self-ignite.

4. When putting paint away, ensure that you close the lid tightly. This prevents oxygen from getting into the tin and forming a skin. If the lid will no longer form a tight seal, you can use cling film to protect the paint. Cover the surface of the paint and the inside wall of the tin with the cling film, then put the lid on top.

5. Paint tins should be stored out of direct sunlight and should be turned every so often.

Brushing out excess paint.

Cleaning a brush with hand soap.

## Use of dark grey or black linseed paint

Historically, many Georgian and Victorian railings were painted with dark grey or black linseed paint. This was not purely for aesthetics. The graphite pigment used in these shades is quite fatty in consistency, which gives a long-lasting finish.

## Chapter Nine

# Masonry, Internal Walls and Other Specialist Applications

Linseed paint is an incredibly versatile material that can be used for painting just about anything. Though it is often associated with wood and metal thanks to its excellent protective properties, it is also regularly used to paint masonry, interior walls and other specialist applications.

## PAINTING MASONRY

Linseed paint has always been a popular choice for painting masonry. This is a traditional option that works brilliantly, especially when compared to the maintenance cycle required when using modern exterior paint. The main reason that linseed paint is a great choice for masonry is the same as the reason it works so well on timber – its wicking properties. When used on masonry, it allows any moisture that is trapped in the substrate to work its way out, rather than penetrating though the wall to the interior surfaces. It will work on all masonry surfaces, including stone, cement, brick and render.

### Preparation

When painting a masonry surface, you will need to take some time to ensure that the surface is ready.

### Checking for damage

To begin with, you must make sure that the surface is free from damp problems and contamination, and that it is in sound condition with no loose rendering. If any areas require attention, these should be dealt with before proceeding.

### Removing paint

If the masonry surface has already been painted with non-linseed paint, the paint will need to be removed for best results. Equally, any synthetic masonry coatings will have to be removed. The best approach is usually to use a paint stripper, followed by a lot of scrubbing and scraping. This is likely to be highly labour-intensive, but will be worth it when you consider the amount of maintenance you will be avoiding in the future. Depending on the type of substrate, you may be able to use a hot pressure washer to assist, but do be careful as these can damage some types of masonry.

In some situations, you may wish to consider a heated steam cleaning system such as the DOFF Integra. These machines heat water to over 150°C (300°F), then eject it as superheated steam. The machine can then be used to remove any existing paint as well as graffiti and any particularly stubborn grime. These machines have been developed for use in restoration work and are safe to use on most types of masonry surface.

### Final preparations

Once you have confirmed that the surface is ready to be worked on, the next step is to remove any nails, screws or other metal objects. This is important as these objects can leave rust stains on the masonry.

Finally, the surface should either be brushed down, or cleaned with linseed soap or brown soap. This is an important step to get rid of any dust, dirt, mould, algae or pollutants.

## Application

Exterior walls should only be painted using a brush, not a roller or paint sprayer. This can result in quite labour-intensive work, but is the only way to make sure that all of the surface area is covered properly. This is particularly important when painting rough surfaces – applying the paint by brush allows it to be worked into every nook and cranny.

On the whole, painting exterior walls is no different from painting linseed on timber. However, you may find the first two coats tricky on a very porous or absorbent masonry surface. This is because these sorts of surfaces sometimes draw the oil out of the paint too quickly. Not only can this make it difficult to achieve nice, even brushstrokes, but it often also leads to the paint being applied too thickly. If you are working with a very absorbent surface (such as soft brick), you can avoid this by using a specially mixed primer coat, consisting of 30 per cent linseed paint to 70 per cent raw linseed oil.

Depending on the surface and how the primer coat goes on, you may wish to do a second primer coat of 50/50 linseed paint/raw linseed oil. Once the absorption starts to lessen and you can achieve a decent brushstroke, you can then apply the paint straight from the tin.

## PAINTING INTERIOR WALLS

Though in recent decades linseed paint has been used more commonly for exterior purposes, this was not always the case. Before the advent of petrochemical and plastic paints, linseed paint was used just as often inside as it was outside.

This book has discussed the many benefits of linseed paint over modern petrochemical alternatives and these all still stand when used for interior purposes. Linseed paint is a highly durable, natural option for interior projects such as skirting boards, kitchen cupboards and built-in shelving. As this paint adheres well to most surfaces, it is even possible to use it to paint floor tiles. Unfortunately, modern paint does have one advantage over linseed paint when used in an interior setting – it dries much more quickly. Without the benefit of fresh air and natural UV light, linseed paint can take up to ten days to cure fully.

It is also important to understand how linseed paint will be affected by UV light – or the lack of it – over time. Painted surfaces that do not see much, or any, natural daylight can yellow over time. This effect will be far more visible on surfaces that have been painted white or off-white. If you are using one of these shades, do be aware that painted areas behind frames or furniture or the inside of cupboard doors may develop a yellow tint over time. The bleaching effect of UV light means that this may be balanced out if furniture and frames are moved around.

## Interior linseed emulsion

Traditional linseed paint can be used on interior walls and will work perfectly well. However, it may not be practical to leave the room for up to ten days for it to dry! The consistency of traditional linseed paint also does not work as well with a roller as the modern petrochemical paints you might be used to.

There are specialist interior linseed paint options available and these might be a more practical choice. Interior linseed emulsion is still based on traditional linseed paints, but has a natural cellulose emulsifier added, along with chalk. This has three benefits:

- It improves drying time.
- It can be used easily with a paint tray and roller.
- It can be sprayed on.

## Lime plaster

If you are painting the inside of an exterior wall without a cavity that has been plastered using lime plaster, it would probably be best to use a lime wash or a clay paint. This is because these types of paints work in conjunction with lime plaster.

Specialist interior linseed paint has a really nice matt finish. Thanks to the linseed oil it contains, it is also wipeable. In fact, it is one of the most durable matt paints on the market. Application by brush will give an appearance of a lime wash or clay paint, while a spray-applied finish will give a more homogeneous even finish, more in line with what you would expect from a modern-day conventional emulsion.

### Preparation

Just as when working with other surfaces, the better your preparation, the better the final result. When working with freshly plastered walls, you must wait until they are fully dry. Once they have completely cured, sand the whole surface with 120 grit sandpaper. If you are working with a wall that has previously been painted, you can paint over this. The best results will be obtained with a spray application.

### Application

Once the surface has been prepared, you are ready to start painting. If you wish to use a roller, the best option is a good-quality microfibre roller with a large pile (ideally 17mm, if you can get it).

1. Open the tin of paint and check whether it has formed a skin. This is completely normal (it just means that some oxygen has got in) and does not affect the rest of the paint. If there is a skin, scrape it off and discard it; do not stir it into the paint.
2. Stir the paint thoroughly to ensure that no pigments are stuck to the bottom of the tin. Ideally, spend about five minutes doing this.
3. If using a roller, pour the amount of paint you will need into a paint tray. If using a brush, you can paint straight from the tin. If using a spray application, start with the spray settings you are used to and adjust up or down according to the test patch.
4. Unlike other types of linseed paint, specialist interior paint should be applied quite thickly. Put plenty on the roller or brush and apply without working it too much. Spray-applied finishes might not cover in one coat, but no more than two will be needed.
5. Paint working away from the light source (the door and windows).
6. Do each wall in one go (that is, do not do all the cutting in with a brush first, then apply the roller). It is fine to do the edges with a brush, but make sure that you only do as much as you can catch up with a roller before the edges start

Sanding an interior plastered wall.

The paint stirred and ready for application.

Cutting in.

Finished dark interior colour by brush.

to dry. This is called working 'wet in wet' and is especially important when painting with a dark colour.

7. The second coat can be applied once the first coat is dry to the touch.

## Drying and curing

Interior linseed paint dries in two stages. The first is the evaporation of the water content, which takes five to six hours. After this time, the paint will usually feel dry to the touch. However, it will still feel reasonably soft and pigmentation may come off in your hand if you wipe up against it. This is because the linseed oil needs to cure fully, which can take up to ten days. Once the paint has fully cured, it will have a matt finish that is completely wipeable.

## OTHER SPECIALIST APPLICATIONS

### Painting interior woodwork

Traditional linseed paint can be an excellent choice for interior woodwork. Not only is it an all-natural option that will help to protect the woodwork, it also provides a very durable finish. This is great for high-traffic pieces such as wooden kitchen cupboards, doors and even floorboards.

For most interior woodwork projects, you can follow the steps in Chapter 7 and achieve great results. The only change you may wish to make is to add around 10–15 per cent of balsam turpentine to every coat, not just the primer. This will help to improve drying time a little, though you will still need to prepare for a wait, even with good weather and plenty of airflow.

If you would prefer to have a matt finish on interior woodwork, you can choose to use specialist interior paint. This will have the advantage of drying more quickly, though it won't be quite as durable. Standard linseed paint will therefore be a better choice for doors or floorboards.

## Painting floors

Standard linseed paint is exceptionally durable and works really well on a variety of floor types. This includes timber, cement and even tiles. Whatever the type of floor you are working with, the best approach will be to follow the same technique as you would when working on wood, that is, to apply the paint in thin coats and build it up. If you plan to paint glazed wall tiles, you will need to degrease them really well before starting. Glazed floor tiles require a light sanding to improve adhesion.

For a clear finish on interior concrete floors or slabs, the best approach is to saturate the floor with

Applying the boiled oil by roller is an easy way to cover a large are. Make sure to not apply it too thickly and wipe off any excess oil.

boiled linseed oil. This is done by cutting in the edges with a brush, then applying the oil to the main area using a roller. Leave this for twenty to thirty minutes, then wipe off any excess to avoid puddles forming. Repeat this application until the concrete cannot absorb any more oil, then begin the painting process.

## Painting wooden decking

Linseed paint is an ideal choice for wooden decking. It will help to protect the decking year on year, thereby cutting down considerably on the amount of time needed to be spent on maintenance. It is usually far more straightforward to paint an area of decking than an interior floor. Not only will it be much easier to avoid walking on the decking for the necessary drying period, the increased natural light will speed up the curing period. Again, make sure to apply the paint in thin coats, building it up until you have the look you are after.

Use a brush around the edges and on joints.

## Chapter Ten

# What to Expect Once a Project is Finished

One of the best things about linseed paint is undoubtedly that it requires far less maintenance than conventional paint. However, that's not to say that it won't need any maintenance at all. There are certain things that you may need to look out and possibly treat for in the period immediately after finishing a project and in the years following.

## ISSUES JUST AFTER PAINTING

### Rain spots

Even if you've done your best to choose a clear day for painting, rain cannot always be avoided. If it rains after you've painted, you may see white spots appearing on the painted surface. This is completely normal while the paint is still curing. There is no need to do anything; the white spots will dry up and disappear once the weather improves and the water droplets evaporate.

### Uneven surfaces or 'bubbling'

As linseed paint absorbs into timber, it will push out any moisture that it comes up against. In addition to water, this wicking process will also push out any chemical residue or resin. These things can remain inside old timber even if it has been fully stripped back to bare. They can also be found inside new timber, especially if it has been treated.

As the linseed paint wicks out any resins or chemicals from inside the wood, the paint can be temporarily compromised. This can result in patchiness, an uneven surface and the paint lifting or bubbling. Though this might seem frustrating when you have just achieved a good finish, it is ultimately a good thing. Once the linseed paint has wicked out all the 'nasties', the timber will be better protected in the future.

If this happens, the best thing is to leave the paint for a couple of months (or over the winter) while the wicking process is completed, then give the whole surface a sand down and apply another coat of paint.

Rain spots.

Bubbling up.

### 'Wrinkling' or a rough finish

Linseed paint does not need to be painted on as thickly as petrochemical paints. In fact, if it is painted on too thickly, this can result in a poor finish, such as visible brushstrokes or an otherwise rough appearance. In some cases, linseed paint that has been applied too thickly will result in 'wrinkling', which is when the paint has a wrinkled appearance and never fully dries.

In these cases, the best course of action is to scrape off the excess paint and sand the surface. Once this has been done, apply a very thin coat of paint to get a nice, even finish.

### Problems drying

One of the downsides of linseed paint is that it does take much longer to dry than the type of paint you might be used to. Ideally, it needs dry conditions and plenty of natural UV light to dry fully. Even when the paint is dry to the touch, it can take weeks or even months for the paint to cure fully, especially if conditions are damp or the surface does not get much direct natural light.

Wrinkling.

## LONGER-TERM ISSUES AND MAINTENANCE

Though linseed paint certainly lasts a lot longer than petrochemical outdoor paint and requires a great deal less maintenance, that does not mean it requires no maintenance at all. In order to get the best from the linseed paint you've applied, you will want to take a little time to look after it. There are a couple of options:

- Add a coat of linseed oil on top of painted surfaces every few years (the exact frequency will depend on which colour paint you have chosen and how much direct sunlight the surface gets).
- Repaint the surface every ten to fifteen years.

Either way, you will definitely not need to strip and repaint the surface completely ever again, unlike if using conventional outdoor paint.

### What to look out for

*The surface becoming more matt*

Though linseed paint has a very nice sheen when freshly painted, this is not supposed to last. In fact, linseed paint will not develop its proper patina for a couple of years. Natural UV light will strip oil from the surface over this time, which will eventually result in the lovely matt finish associated with linseed paint. This is a good thing, as, during this process, the steam diffusion (SD) value of the paint (which is a scale for measuring how open a material is) will fall from 70+ to close to 0. The closer to 0 the SD number, the more open the material and the better the wicking process it is able to manage. Do bear in mind, though, that the test for SD values is for the breathability of paint, in particular interior wall paint. True linseed oil paint will be able to wick out moisture even at a higher SD value.

A great example of paint going matte over time.

For this reason, repainting linseed paint too regularly can actually be detrimental, no matter how tempting it might be to try to hold on to the freshly painted sheen of the paint. However, you may wish to add a coat of linseed oil to the surface every few years to keep the paint job and the colour looking fresh.

## The surface becoming powdery or chalky

It is reasonably normal for the surface layer of linseed paint to turn dull, powdery or chalky. This is especially likely to happen in very hot weather, or if the surface in question is particularly exposed to the elements. Do remember that whatever is happening on the top layer, it is still acting as a protective barrier for the timber underneath. This process is often more visible on darker colours, blue in particular. In some cases, the top layer of paint may turn a chalky white colour and come off on your hands. If this happens, there is a simple solution – wiping the surface down with some linseed oil is usually enough to restore the surface layer.

## Colours fading

Just as linseed paint should be expected to develop more of a matt finish over time, you should also expect some changes in the colour of the paint. Some pigments will be more colour-fast than others, so if this is something that concerns you, it may be worth doing a bit more research before starting your project. The important part is that any colour shift or change is unlikely to have an impact on the function of the paint. Slight colour changes often occur as part of the process of UV light stripping oil over time, but this process is not detrimental to the effectiveness of the paint.

White and off-white colours tend to look fresh the longest. If your surface is affected by pollen or traffic pollution this may temporarily discolour it, but a good clean with some linseed soap once a year will be sufficient.

Reds, yellows, browns, greys and blacks usually require the least amount of maintenance. As a rule, you would not normally need to re-oil these colours for seven to eight years, depending on conditions.

This board shows faded or matted Chatsworth Blue (centre). To the left is a fresh coat of paint and to the right is what one coat of boiled oil looks like.

Blue and dark green shades are the hardest to keep fresh. In these shades, the oil makes the pigments appear darker, so as this is stripped away the tint will look lighter. This can be resolved easily enough with a fresh coat of oil, but to keep a blue shade looking its best – especially if it is on a surface that gets a lot of direct light – you may need to re-oil every year.

## Mould developing

Good-quality linseed paint should include zinc pigments. Zinc, along with the protection from trapped moisture afforded by linseed paint, does help to combat the growth of mould. However, this does not mean that you won't still need to keep up with other anti-mould strategies. Keep an eye out for any standing water on the paintwork and also regularly wipe away any debris, dust or dirt.

If mould does appear as time goes on, in the first instance the best thing to do is to spray the mould with white vinegar, leave it for twenty-four hours, then brush the mould off and rinse the area with water.

Mouldy window.

## Re-Oiling

Re-oiling your painted surfaces is simple. Start by giving the surface a good clean with linseed soap, making sure to remove any algae. Once the surface is clean and dry, wipe on a thin coat of good-quality raw linseed oil. Depending on environmental conditions, the colour of the paint and your personal preferences, you may wish to do this as often as once a year, or as infrequently as once every eight years. The more regularly you do it, the less frequently you will need to repaint.

## Chapter Eleven

# Frequently Asked Questions

## GENERAL QUESTIONS

### Is linseed paint expensive?

Considering the many benefits of linseed paint, you may be expecting it to be more expensive than other options. It is true that you might find it more expensive per can than mainstream paints, but that isn't the whole story. Why? Because another significant benefit of linseed paint is that it has much better coverage than modern paints.

Modern paints are made of water, plastic, synthetic colourants, drying agents and emulsifiers. High-quality linseed paint contains only linseed oil and pigments. This is why a tin of linseed paint weighs twice as much as an equivalent-sized tin of modern paint and why it goes significantly further. Therefore, you will pay less per metre-squared painted with linseed paint than you would with a modern alternative. It is also worth taking into account that linseed paint will not need to be reapplied every few years like many other types of paint.

The cost of high-quality linseed paint is related to the manufacturing process. To make linseed paint properly, triple roller mills are required in order to disperse the powder pigments evenly into the oil. Though it is possible to make linseed paint more cheaply by stirring rather than milling it, this simply does not work as well. It really is worth paying the extra for a top-quality product.

### Is linseed paint breathable?

Linseed paint is not breathable in the same way as lime paint, which lets moisture in and out again.

Instead, linseed paint allows moisture to wick out, but does not let it in.

### Is there an ideal time of year for applying linseed paint?

If you are using linseed paint outside, it is helpful to consider the environmental conditions before you get started. There is no minimum temperature for the paint to be applied successfully, so, theoretically speaking, you could paint outside even in the depths of winter. However, humidity levels can affect both how well the paint will adhere to the surface and how long it will take to dry.

Ideally, it is best to use linseed paint when the surface you are painting is completely dry, the air humidity levels are low, there is minimal risk of rainfall and there is plenty of good UV light. These factors are most likely to be in your favour during the spring and summer months.

Of course, things do not always work out perfectly and it may be the case that a surface needs to be painted during the autumn or winter. You can still paint during these times, but it will take much longer for the paint to dry and fully cure. In these situations, I would recommend applying a primer coat of linseed paint to the exposed surface in order to protect it, then waiting until the weather improves to add further coats.

### How long should linseed paint last?

Linseed paint should last for ten to fifteen years before it needs to be repainted.

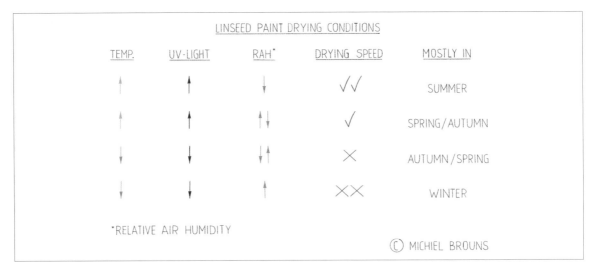

| LINSEED PAINT DRYING CONDITIONS | | | | |
|---|---|---|---|---|
| TEMP. | UV-LIGHT | RAH* | DRYING SPEED | MOSTLY IN |
| ↑ | ↑ | ↓ | ✓✓ | SUMMER |
| ↑ | ↑ | ↑↓ | ✓ | SPRING/AUTUMN |
| ↓ | ↓ | ↓↑ | ✕ | AUTUMN/SPRING |
| ↓ | ↓ | ↑ | ✕✕ | WINTER |

*RELATIVE AIR HUMIDITY

Ⓒ MICHIEL BROUNS

When to paint with linseed paint.

## Will UV light affect the colour of linseed paint over time?

Linseed paint generally offers a level of UV protection. Some pigments will not be as stable as others over time, so this should be taken into account when choosing your shade.

## Does linseed paint always prevent mould and rot?

In order to help prevent mould and mildew, linseed paint needs to contain the pigment zinc white. If you use linseed paint containing the correct amount of zinc white, it should prevent mould in normal conditions. However, mould can still sometimes occur if there is standing water, if the linseed paint hasn't adhered to the surface properly, or if it was not applied directly to the wood.

## Should linseed paint contain raw or boiled linseed oil?

High-quality linseed paint should always be made with boiled linseed oil. Boiling linseed oil before it is made into paint makes it more durable and improves drying times.

## Can you mix pigments into linseed oil yourself?

This is not recommended, as the most effective way to add pigments to linseed oil is during a process of triple roller milling. However, if you want to achieve a certain colour, you could buy multiple colours of linseed paint and mix them together.

## SAFETY QUESTIONS

## Does linseed paint contain lead?

No, modern linseed paint does not contain lead. Historically, many types of linseed paint would have contained the pigment lead white, which is highly toxic. Nowadays, zinc white is used instead, which offers the same anti-mould benefits without any risk of lead poisoning.

## Is linseed paint or oil flammable?

Linseed paint itself is not flammable and is perfectly safe to use. However, you do need to be careful when working with linseed oil and linseed paint in its wet state. There is a small risk that any rags that have been used during the painting process could be flammable, so it is important to soak them in water before disposing of them.

Is linseed paint safe for babies and toddlers?

Linseed paint is safe to be used in the home and there are no concerns about using it around babies and young children generally. However, you should carefully consider whether to paint a wooden cot or any other item that a baby may chew on, as some of the pigments used, including zinc white, are not intended to be ingested.

Is linseed paint safe to use inside stables?

Linseed paint is safe to use inside stables, as it is non-toxic and contains no solvents or phthalates. The only smell the paint will give off is of linseed oil and as this is often fed to horses, they will likely already be used to the scent.

Is linseed paint safe to use on beehives?

Yes, linseed paint is often used on beehives. The paint is non-toxic and has no known adverse effects on bee health.

## SUITABILITY QUESTIONS

Can linseed paint be used inside?

Yes, linseed paint can be used inside. However, it can take quite a long time to dry, especially inside where there is less natural sunlight. Depending on the situation, this might not be very practical. Some linseed paint manufacturers make specialist interior ranges with added drying agents to combat this.

Can linseed paint be used on newly plastered walls?

Yes, there are types of linseed paint that are made specifically for use on new plaster. You will just need to ensure that the plaster is fully dry before you begin. If the plaster is new, it may require an extra coat or so of paint.

Can linseed paint be used on lime-plastered walls?

Linseed paint can be used on lime-plastered walls, though in these cases it might make more sense to use a lime wash or lime paint.

Can linseed paint be used on metal?

Yes, linseed paint works well on metal surfaces such as railings and radiators. For best results, use a linseed-based iron oxide primer designed to prevent rust, then two coats of linseed paint over the top.

Can linseed paint be used on untreated wood?

Linseed paint is very effective when used on untreated wood. I would recommend starting with a diluted primer coat to ensure that the paint fully penetrates the timber.

Can linseed paint be used on varnished hardwood?

You can use linseed paint on hardwood that has previously been varnished. In order to get the full benefit of the linseed paint, you will need to remove as much of the varnish as possible prior to painting.

Can linseed paint be used on masonry?

Masonry is an ideal surface for linseed paint. Ensure that all previous paint has been removed from the masonry, then apply the linseed paint in very thin coats.

Can linseed paint be used on tiles?

Linseed paint will adhere to most types of tiles. Make sure that they have been thoroughly degreased and rubbed down first.

## Can linseed paint be used on MDF?

Linseed paint will work well on MDF surfaces. If the MDF is bare, you should start with a primer coat (50 per cent linseed paint mixed with 35 per cent boiled linseed oil and 15 per cent balsam turpentine). If the MDF is laminated, you can paint the first coat straight from the tin (though I would advise giving the laminated surface a light key and a good degreasing first).

## Can linseed paint be used on lead flashing?

I would not recommend using linseed paint on lead flashing. It will not adhere well and is therefore unlikely to last very long.

## Can linseed paint be used over silicone/silicon?

If you are painting a surface with joints filled with silicone or silicon, linseed paint should cover these well. Make sure that you use thin, even coats.

## Can linseed paint be used over fillers, substrates and putties?

Linseed paint will adhere to pretty much every substrate, filler and putty, so there should be no problem overpainting. Make sure that any fillers and substrates are completely dry before painting to avoid a reaction. If using linseed putty, generally you will just need to wait until it has formed a skin before you paint it.

## Can linseed paint be used on uPVC?

Linseed paint adheres well to uPVC and can be a great way to get a more attractive or historical look without the expense or waste of replacing windows. However, it is really important for linseed paint not to come into direct contact with double-glazing seals, as it will damage them. To avoid this, apply one coat of acrylic paint over the seals, wait for this to dry completely, then apply linseed paint over the top.

## Can linseed paint be used to paint kitchen units?

Absolutely. Linseed paint is a hardwearing paint that will stand up well on kitchen cupboards. For best results, I would suggest following the same steps as you would with any other timber application, including removing all existing paint and starting with a primer coat. If you wanted to ensure that cabinets are extra protected, you could finish with a coat of a linseed oil-based varnish such as Le Tonkinois.

## Can linseed paint be used to paint floors?

Yes, linseed paint should stand up well on wooden, tiled or concrete floors. It can also work well on stairs. Interior floors are likely to need a reasonably long time to dry, so make sure you have planned for this. If painting stairs, you may wish to paint alternate treads so that the stairs are still accessible.

## Can linseed paint be used to paint boats?

Linseed paint was traditionally used to paint wooden boats, so it has an excellent track record going back hundreds of years. The best tried and tested method is to use two to three coats of linseed paint, then six to eight coats of linseed varnish such as Le Tonkinois. This also works well on metal boats.

## PREPARATION QUESTIONS

### How should a wooden surface be prepared for linseed paint?

Before painting a wooden surface, you will need to make sure that it is completely dry. You will also need to sand off any paint, oils or primers that have previously been applied. If you are painting untreated timber, start with a primer coat made of a solution of 50 per cent linseed paint, 35 per cent boiled linseed oil and 15 per cent balsam turpentine.

## How should a metal surface be prepared for linseed paint?

Before painting a metal surface, you will need to make sure that you have removed any rust and thoroughly cleaned it. The best way to do this is to use a steel wire brush and then clean the whole surface with a degreasing solution such as sugar soap.

## Does all previous paint have to be removed before linseed oil can be applied?

Whatever surface you are painting, best practice would be to remove any previous modern paint before applying linseed paint. Though this might seem like unnecessary extra work, it will enable you to get the full benefit from the linseed paint. If there is existing paint on the surface, the wicking properties of the linseed paint will be compromised. Any flaking of the old paint may also cause the linseed paint to flake.

In some situations, it might not be possible to remove all previous traces of paint. You can still use linseed paint in these scenarios, but be aware that it might not be as effective or long-lasting.

## When should linseed paint be applied after a surface has been prepared?

For best results, leave a prepared surface to dry completely before repainting with linseed paint. If you are working with a wooden surface, this is likely to take longer than you think! In many cases, you will need to leave a surface for six to eight weeks to allow any moisture to disperse fully.

## Should raw linseed oil be applied to wood before painting with linseed paint?

There is no benefit to using raw linseed oil as a primer. In fact, it can be detrimental. Linseed oil does not offer any mould or mildew protection when used on its own; it needs to be combined with pigments to provide this. Painting a wooden surface with linseed oil will simply saturate the timber and mean that any linseed paint applied over the top will not be able to penetrate the surface properly. Linseed paint that cannot adhere properly will not be able to protect the surface as efficiently. There is also a risk that saturating a timber surface with linseed oil will cause it to crack when it dries out, especially if the oil has been heated.

## Can linseed paint be used on a surface that has been stripped with Peelaway or other chemical treatments?

There is usually no problem painting a surface after paint-stripping chemicals have been used. However, you will need to ensure that the surface has been thoroughly cleaned and neutralised afterwards. If there is any residue left, it may react with the linseed paint.

## APPLICATION QUESTIONS

### Should the first coat of linseed paint be diluted with linseed oil?

In some situations, there is a benefit to starting with a primer coat, which is where the linseed paint is diluted with raw linseed oil and balsam turpentine. This is particularly helpful when painting untreated timber, as the primer stabilises the absorption levels and allows the combination of oil and pigment to penetrate into the timber more deeply. I would also recommend a primer coat for oily or exotic hardwoods.

To make this primer solution, mix a solution of 50 per cent linseed paint, 35 per cent raw linseed oil and 15 per cent balsam turpentine. After this first coat has been applied, the following coats can be painted straight from the tin, with no dilution necessary.

### How many coats of linseed paint are needed?

For most projects, I would recommend three thin coats of linseed paint. When refreshing a surface that has previously been painted with linseed paint, usually only one coat is needed.

### Can linseed paint be applied with a spray gun?

The traditional linseed paint cannot be applied with a spray gun as that will cause the paint to form a film on the surface. The inferior linseed paint described earlier can be applied by spray gun.

### Should the front and back of wood be painted to get the full protective effect?

If you are painting wooden surfaces such as soffits or facias, you may wonder if you should paint both the front and the back. If you can do so before the wood is placed in situ, this would be ideal. However, this isn't always possible, so painting just the exposed side will provide a fair level of protection.

### How long does linseed paint take to dry?

All factors being ideal, each coat of linseed paint will take around twenty-four hours to dry. Painting thin coats will help, as will making sure that you have chosen a dry day to paint and that there's plenty of bright natural sunlight (linseed paint likes to have plenty of UV light while curing).

If you are using linseed paint inside where there is not as much natural light, or if drying conditions outside are not ideal, you should factor extra drying time into your plan. In some circumstances, it could take up to seventy-two hours for linseed paint to dry.

### Is there any way to speed up the drying time?

The best way to ensure a reasonable drying time is to choose a time of year when there is lots of natural UV light and a forecast period of three to four days of good weather. If this is not possible, or if you have a reason to speed up the drying time, there are a few things that might help.

Balsam turpentine can improve drying times, so starting with a primer coat that includes this will help. You can also add 5–10 per cent balsam turpentine to the second coat, but ideally the third coat should be painted undiluted, straight from the tin. UV lights and heaters can also help to speed up drying time, especially inside.

It is important to note, however, that the general rule is that the longer the paint takes to dry, the more durable it will be. Adding too much balsam turpentine or other drying agents can therefore compromise the durability and elasticity of the paint. If you need to paint at a time of year that is not ideal in terms of drying times, you could also choose to paint just the primer coat initially and then wait to apply subsequent coats once the weather is more suitable.

### Can linseed oil be used to coat/protect natural timber?

Linseed oil will not protect natural timber by itself; it is the combination of the oil and pigments that protects against mould and mildew. However, if you want to get all the benefits of linseed paint while still retaining a natural wood look, there are specialist linseed oil products available for this. They will usually need to be reapplied every two to three years. You could also consider using pine tar oil.

### What can be done to stop paint bleeding?

In some cases, linseed paint may bleed a small amount, especially when used on newer timber. This can be more pronounced with white paint. You can try using shellac to remove any areas of bleeding.

### How should paint drips be removed?

Ideally, paint drips should be wiped away as soon as they occur. If you miss any, they can be taken off with sandpaper once dry. If you find that the paint is dripping a lot, this may be because you are applying the coat too thickly.

## How should brushes be cared for during and after applying linseed paint?

For best results, good-quality brushes should be used. This makes it even more important to care for them properly. Brushes can be kept in water overnight with no adverse effect, which is great if you are halfway through a project. If you need to pause for a longer period, leave them stored in raw linseed oil.

Once you have finished painting, the best way to clean your brushes is with a mild detergent or linseed oil soap.

## Can linseed paint spills be removed from clothing?

If you spill any linseed paint on your clothes, act quickly! If the paint is still wet, you should be able to get it off using linseed oil soap, or water and a mild detergent. If the paint has dried, it is more difficult to get off clothes and you may not have much success.

## How can skin on linseed paint be removed?

If a tin of linseed paint has been left open for too long, it may develop a skin on the surface. If this happens, do not stir the skin into the paint. Instead, lift out the skin and discard. You can avoid this in future by putting cling film over the paint, then putting the lid on top.

## MAINTENANCE QUESTIONS

## How long can linseed paint be kept or stored?

Linseed paint can be kept indefinitely. Assuming an opened can of paint is stored correctly, you should be able to use it years later. Just make sure to remove any skin and give it a thorough mix before use.

## How should linseed paint be stored?

Tins should be kept tightly sealed. In order to prevent oxidation, you can put cling film over the top before refitting the lid. Ideally, the tins of any stored paint should be turned every few months.

## Why might white linseed paint yellow over time?

If white linseed paint is applied to a surface that gets no natural UV light, it may develop a creamy yellow tint over time. This should only happen if the surface gets no natural light at all, for instance on the inside of a cupboard door. In these situations, white might not be a good colour choice if you want the colour to remain stable over time.

## What if the paint blisters?

Occasionally, linseed paint applied to timber might blister. On old timber, this might be due to traces of old products or chemicals that have stayed within the wood (this can occur no matter how well the wood was stripped prior to painting). On new timber, it is often due to the wood having a high resin content.

Though this may seem like an annoyance, it is actually a good thing. As the linseed paint absorbs into the timber, it will push out any moisture within. This process, called wicking, might take a few months to complete. After this time, you will be able to sand down any blisters and paint on a final coat.

## How should a surface be prepared to reapply linseed paint?

Rub the surface down, then apply linseed paint directly from the tin.

## Chapter Twelve

# Linseed Paint: Past, Present and Future

The reality of the time we live in is that we all need to consider carefully the materials we are using in terms of our impact on the environment. This book has set out many reasons for choosing linseed paint over more contemporary alternatives. However, perhaps one of the most pressing reasons going forwards is because of environmental concerns. All the big paint companies use plastic in the manufacture of their paint, even in so-called eco or historical ranges.

Linseed paint, however, is different. Traditionally made linseed paints do not contain any plastics at all and can therefore be considered a much more environmentally sustainable choice. Perhaps what we're looking at here is the process of linseed paint coming full circle – aside from a hiatus of seventy or eighty years, it had been used uninterrupted for many centuries.

Linseed paint is still largely a labour-intensive product to make and apply. The care that goes into the growing of the flax, the harvesting of the seeds, the boiling of the oil, the selection of the powder earth pigments and the grinding of the pigments into the oil are all very deliberate and add soul. The fact that linseed paint is made with such care and attention should do good; good for the decorator, good for the building and good for the occupants.

## THE PROBLEMS WITH PLASTIC PAINT

The US Environmental Protection Agency has highlighted the role that plastic paint plays in what it considers to be the most significant environmental hazards.[48] Even long after it has dried, typical plastic paint will continue to release petroleum-based solvents called volatile organic compounds (VOCs). Over time, these VOCs can turn the air inside our homes and workplaces into chemical cocktails.

The majority of conventional paints available from big manufacturers are essentially all the same product – synthetic colourants mixed into acrylics and/or latex. Not only does this lead to more by-products, more waste and more unsustainable manufacturing processes, plastic paint results in huge amounts of plastic getting into our water sources.

Every time that acrylic paints are washed off brushes, cleared out of paint trays, or rinsed from rags, more plastic particles are washed down our drains. From there, they work their way into rivers, seas and oceans. A recent Environmental Action study shows that the biggest source of plastic pollution in the ocean is not from single-use plastics but from acrylic paint derivatives, which account for about 58 per cent of microplastics in the oceans.[49]

Of course, once plastics are in our water sources, it does not take long for them to get into our bodies. The University of Amsterdam has published results in *Science Direct* about how, for the first time ever, it has located and identified plastic particles in human blood samples.[50]

### Greenwashing

Greenwashing refers to the process of brands (mostly big, well-known ones) attempting to piggyback the movement towards the use of more environmentally friendly products and application methods. This happens throughout the consumer world, but it seems to be particularly rife in the building industry.

Many big players in the paint industry have employed these kinds of tactics. Most have started producing so-called 'green' product lines that boast low VOCs, or claim to be water-based. Unfortunately, there is really no such thing as a water-based acrylic paint. Though it may be possible to dilute these paints with water, they are absolutely not water-based in the same way that lime washes, distempers and clay paints are. As for manufacturers lowering VOC levels, unfortunately the only real way to do this with a petrochemical paint is to replace the VOCs with alternative phthalates, weakeners and emulsifiers. Phthalates are a known carcinogenic. The majority of these chemicals are no healthier than what they are replacing and may very well be banned themselves in another few decades because of how toxic they are. There have also been times when big paint manufacturers have added a small amount of linseed oil to their paints, but of course a small percentage of a natural ingredient cannot make the whole product natural.

Though there is undoubtedly commercial benefit to these big companies producing greenwashed products, we cannot realistically expect plastic paint manufacturers to develop a solution to the problem. Rather, their business model relies on them producing 'new' solutions every now and again, while using mainly the same low-cost, petrochemical-derived ingredients.

### Considering paint as a building product

Before the plastic revolution of the mid-twentieth century, paint was predominantly viewed as a building product. Unlike today, when paint is usually viewed solely as an aesthetic decor product, paint was generally understood to be a sacrificial layer to protect whatever surface was beneath it.

Perhaps a lot of the problems concerning harmful plastic paints would be solved if we went back to considering paint as a building product. If paint was to be regarded as a key structural element of our buildings, we would need to consider more carefully what it was made of. This could well help to address one of the biggest necessities of our time – using less plastic. It would also go a long way towards letting our buildings breathe, thereby reducing mould, humidity and the number of timber repairs.

The true solution here relies on using the correct, low-carbon ingredients. This is unlikely to be something adopted freely by big paint manufacturers, because low-carbon ingredients such as linseed oil tend to be more expensive, as is the labour involved in processing them. However, the reality here is that if the building industry keeps buying the same, low-cost, high-margin products with built-in obsolescence, nothing will ever change.

## OTHER ENVIRONMENTAL CONCERNS

There is no doubt that reducing plastic must become a priority for the building industry, but there is a range of other issues that also needs addressing.

### Embodied energy

The concept of embodied energy has not yet reached mainstream understanding, but it has been a consideration in parts of the architectural world for some time already. Essentially, it is the question of how much energy is needed for the manufacture and transport of each material. The embodied energy of a material must be taken into account when considering how sustainable and environmentally friendly a product is.

Contemporary paint does not generally perform well in this category, as its base tends to be made from acrylics and latex, both of which are derived from crude oil. However, linseed paint is different. Linseed oil is obtained by cold-pressing flaxseed, which does not require energy-intensive heat or refineries. The oil is then combined with raw earth pigments (generally obtained during a relatively low-energy process of daylight mining) and mixed by a triple mill roller, which does not require a huge amount of energy to run. This whole process means that linseed paint has a far lower embodied energy cost than conventional paint.

In fact, the biggest contribution to the embodied energy of linseed paint is in the packing and transport. A related issue here is the question of product miles. The fewer product miles each item has, the lower its embodied energy will be. This is something that more environmentally responsible manufacturers put a lot of thought into, but no doubt there is always space for improvement.

### Cradle to cradle products

The holy grail of environmentally sustainable building materials would be a product that leaves no impact on the environment from the moment it is conceived, to manufacture, to supply, to use, to being recycled or reabsorbed by Mother Earth. This concept is called cradle to cradle. Linseed paint is a fantastic candidate for a cradle to cradle-certified product.

There is an internationally recognised cradle to cradle accreditation programme, but unfortunately this already seems to have fallen foul of capitalism. The cost of getting accreditation starts at £10,000, which is not accessible to smaller, independent businesses that are doing great work with sustainable products. Hopefully this will change in the near future to support products on the basis of how they actually perform rather than how much cash can be spent on them.

## IS LINSEED PAINT THE HEALTHIER OPTION?

The environments we live in are an important factor in our health and well-being. Unfortunately, our understanding of this in the UK and the USA seems to be years behind the curve. Scandinavian countries, as well as Australia and New Zealand, have already done a lot of research into this topic. Thanks to them, we have a great deal more insight into so-called 'sick building syndrome' than we would otherwise.

Sick building syndrome encapsulates the theory that our homes are majorly impacted by chemical contaminants and electromagnetic radiation. Everything from the VOCs in paint (or chemicals used to reduce VOC content) to chemicals used in processing flooring, furniture and decor combine to have a major impact on how healthy our home environments are to live in.[51]

Paint, of course, is a significant consideration here. Petrochemical paints can give off toxic chemicals for up to five years after application. Clearly, we should be considering more natural paint products like linseed paint not only for the benefit of buildings, but also for ourselves, our families and our pets.

### Mould reduction

Linseed paint is particularly valuable when used in older properties. Buildings with solid wall structures and/or built-in timber are particularly susceptible to mould when modern, non-breathable paints are used. Choosing a paint that has wicking properties or is breathable can make a huge difference, not just to the structural integrity of the building, but also to the health of the people who live in it.

Both the World Health Organisation (WHO) and the US National Institute of Health's National Library of Medicine (NIH/NLM) recommend that work and living environments should be free of fungi and mould. This is because their presence can have serious impacts on our health. According to the WHO:

Sufficient epidemiological evidence is available from studies conducted in different countries and under different climatic conditions to show that the occupants of damp or mouldy buildings, both houses and public buildings, are at increased risk of respiratory symptoms, respiratory infections and exacerbation of asthma. Some evidence suggests increased risks of allergic rhinitis and asthma.[52]

Unfortunately, building regulations do not generally emphasise the importance of choosing building materials that are designed to protect against the build-up of condensation and damp. Wicking, breathable paint like linseed paint is not a perfect solution to the problem of mould and fungi, but it can play an important part of a holistic approach to managing the humidity levels in your home.

### Dealing with humidity

Old houses often get dismissed with the label 'cold and damp'. However, this does not necessarily have to be the case. Though it can be a bit more of an effort to avoid the problem of humidity in an older building, it is certainly not just something that has to be accepted. This area is often perceived as rather complex, but that is not necessarily the case.

Essentially, airflow and ventilation are vital for keeping both the fabric of a building intact and ensuring that the spaces inside remain healthy. When considering airflow, it might help to think in terms of 'dew points'. These are the points within a building where water vapour settles and turns into dew, or droplets when it settles as water in a liquid state. In older houses, the most common dew points are single-glazed windows (which are typically the place where the difference between the inside and outside air temperatures is the highest).

Good airflow is absolutely critical to achieve a healthy humidity level. It is also helpful to understand that warm air can carry a lot more moisture than cool air. Because of this, instead of draught-proofing and insulating our homes, it can actually be a lot more effective to open windows for a short, sharp fifteen-minute burst during cooler weather.

Even if it's wet outside, the cold air flowing in will contain significantly less moisture than the warm air flowing out.

Another key way to help maintain a stable humidity level is to ensure that the walls can both absorb moisture when required *and* release it again. Breathable and wicking paints can play a crucial role here. The ultimate guide to this is *The Warm Dry Home, A Practical Guide to Understanding the Causes and Solutions of Damp in Buildings* by Pete Ward.[53]

## MAKING YOUR CHOICE

The idea of making a meaningful difference to the planet can feel hopeless, especially when governments and big corporations seem to be doing very little. Real, systemic change in the building industry needs a huge amount of political capital and for developers to reassess their business strategies completely.

However, big systemic change is not the only tool in our arsenal. The answer could well lie in the accumulated effort of what we can do on a small scale. We do not have to wait for industrial conglomerates to tell us what is right and what is wrong.

Most of us only get one or two opportunities in our lifetime to build a house or undertake a big renovation. Whether we are attempting to maintain an old property or build a new one, the wisest choice here is surely to consider how this can be done with as small a carbon impact as possible. Not only is this for the good of the environment, it also has a knock-on effect for the people and pets who live, work or socialise in the building.

Even if we are taking on much smaller projects, we always have a choice about the type of products to use, the companies to buy them from and the long-term sustainability we hope to achieve. These choices will have a direct impact on us, as well as the many generations we hope will come after us.

Choose wisely, my friends. Choose wisely and make a difference for the better.

## Introduction

[1] Mayes, T.M., *Why Old Places Matter* (Lanham, MD: Rowman & Littlefield, 2018)

[2] Eggen, C., *Vakwerkbouw* (Nijmegen: Vantilt, 2016)

[3] https://www.sciencedirect.com/topics/agricultural-and-biological-sciences/linum-usitatissimum

[4] Eggen, *Vakwerkbouw*

## Chapter 1

[5] https://www.channel4.com/press/news/egyptologist-unearths-clues-tutankhamuns-botched-mummification

[6] Smith, J., *The Art of Painting in Oyl* (London: J. Bew, 1723)

[7] Keller, K.W., 'From the Rhineland to the Virginia Frontier: Flax Production as a Commercial Enterprise', *The Virginia Magazine of History and Biography*, Vol. 98, No. 3 (Richmond, VA: Virginia Historical Society, 1990)

[8] Keller, 'From the Rhineland to the Virginia Frontier: Flax Production as a Commercial Enterprise'

[9] Smith, *The Art of Painting in Oyl*

[10] Keller, 'From the Rhineland to the Virginia Frontier: Flax Production as a Commercial Enterprise'

[11] Philbrik, N., *Mayflower* (London: The Folio Society, 2019)

[12] Deetz, P. and Deetz, S., *The Times of their Lives: Life, Love, and Death in Plymouth Colony* (New York: W.H. Freeman, 2002)

[13] Keller, 'From the Rhineland to the Virginia Frontier: Flax Production as a Commercial Enterprise'

[14] https://historicengland.org.uk/get-involved/visit/shrewsbury-flax-mill/

[15] Keller, 'From the Rhineland to the Virginia Frontier: Flax Production as a Commercial Enterprise'

## Chapter 2

[16] https://claessons.com/lite-om-trätjära

[17] Robinson, N., Evershed, P.P., Higgs, J.W. *et al.*, 'Proof of a Pine Wood Origin for Pitch from Tudor (*Mary Rose*) and Etruscan Shipwrecks: Application of Analytical Organic Chemistry in Archaeology', *Analyst*, 1987

[18] Egenberg, I.M., *Tarring Maintenance of Norwegian Medieval Stave Churches* (Göteborg Acta Universitatis Gothoburgensis, 2003)

[19] Robinson *et al.*, 'Proof of a Pine Wood Origin for Pitch from Tudor (*Mary Rose*) and Etruscan Shipwrecks: Application of Analytical Organic Chemistry in Archaeology'

[20] Carson, C. and Lounsbury, C. (eds), *The Chesapeake House – Architectural Investigation by Colonial Williamsburg* (Chapel Hill, NC: University of North Carolina Press, 2013)

[21] Egenberg, *Tarring Maintenance of Norwegian Medieval Stave Churches*

## Chapter 3

[22] McCaig, I. and Ridout, B., *English Heritage Practical Building Conservation – Timber* (Oxford: Routledge, 2018)

[23] Ridout, B., *Timber Decay in Buildings and its Treatment* (London: Historic England, 2019)

[24] https://my.clevelandclinic.org/health/diseases/14770-aspergillosis

[25] https://www.canadabay.nsw.gov.au/community/community-services/the-rhodes-peninsula/rhodes-history

[26] Källbom, A., *Painting Treatments of Weather-Exposed Ferrous Heritage* (Gothenburg: University of Gothenburg, 2021)

## Chapter 4

[27] Carson and Lounsbury, *The Chesapeake House – Architectural Investigation by Colonial Williamsburg*

[28] Boogert, A., *300 Years Before Color* (Madrid: The Galobart Books, 2021)

[29] Albers, J., *Interaction in Color* (New Haven, CT: Yale University Press, 2013)

[30] Church, A.H., *The Chemistry of Paints and Painting* (London: Seeley and Co. Ltd, 1890)

[31] https://blogs.ucl.ac.uk/pigment-timeline/2020/03/25

[32] http://www.webexhibits.org/pigments/indiv/history/tiwhite.html

[33] https://www.nytimes.com/2015/08/19/arts/international/lapis-lazuli-and-the-history-of-the-most-perfect-color.html

[34] *A Treatise and General Primer on the Properties of Early American Paints* (Historic Paints Ltd, 1994)

[35] *Binnenstad*, 273, November/December 2015, the magazine of the VVAB, loosely translated as the 'Friends of Amsterdam's Old Town'

## Chapter 5

[36] *The English Heritage Practical Building Conservation Guide on Timber* (Oxford: Routledge, 2018)

[37] Ridout, B., *Timber Decay in Buildings and its Treatment* (London: Historic England, 2019)

[38] Drewett, T., *The Growth and Quality of UK-Grown Douglas-Fir* (Edinburgh: Edinburgh Napier University, 2015)

[39] Drewett, *The Growth and Quality of UK-Grown Douglas-Fir*

[40] *The English Heritage Practical Building Conservation Guide on Timber*

[41] https://www.accoya.com/faq/how-is-accoya-wood-made/

[42] https://www.greenbuildingadvisor.com/article/the-rise-and-fall-of-a-miracle-wood

[43] http://ports.com/sea-route

## Chapter 6

[44] Ullmann, F., *Ullmann's Encyclopedia of Industrial Chemistry* (Rastede: Wiley-VCH, 1994)

## Chapter 7

[45] IVF Industrial Research and Development Institute in Mölndal tested the Speedheater infrared guns in 2005/06

## Chapter 8

[46] IVF Industrial Research and Development Institute in Mölndal tested the Speedheater infrared guns in 2005/06

[47] Källbom, *Painting Treatments of Weather-Exposed Ferrous Heritage*

## Chapter 12

[48] https://www.neefusa.org/health/asthma/health-impacts-indoor-air-quality#:~:text=Currently%2C%20indoor%20air%20pollution%20is,mold%2C%20and%20second%20hand%20smoke

[49] Paruta, P., *et al.*, *Plastic Paints the Environment; A global assessment of paint's contribution to plastic leakage to land, ocean & waterways* (Lausanne: Environmental Action, 2021)

[50] https://www.sciencedirect.com/science/article/pii/S0160412022001258

[51] Joshi, S.M., 'The Sick Building Syndrome', *Indian Journal of Occupational and Environmental Medicine*, vol. 12, 2 (2008), pp 61–4. doi:10.4103/0019-5278.43262

[52] World Health Organisation, *WHO Guidelines for Indoor Air Quality* (WHO Regional Office Europe, 2009), https://www.euro.who.int/data/assets/pdf_file/0017/43325/E92645.pdf

[53] Ward, P., *The Warm Dry Home, A Practical Guide to Understanding the Causes and Solutions of Damp in Buildings* (Marlborough, Wilts: The Crowood Press, 2022)

Baty, P., *The Anatomy of Colour* (London: Thames & Hudson, 2017)

Bernstein, F.A., *Princeton University School of Architecture, Lecture: Negative Energy and (Dis)Embodied Carbon* https://soa.princeton.edu/node/3072

Boulboullé, J. (2019), drawn up by a learned physician from the mouths of artisans, *Netherlands Yearbook for History of Art / Nederlands Kunsthistorisch Jaarboek Online*, 68(1), 204-249. doi: https://doi.org/10.1163/22145966-06801008

Bristow, I.C., *Architectural Colour in British Interiors 1615–1840* (New Haven, CT: Yale University Press, 1996)

Church, A.H., *The Chemistry of Paints and Painting* (London, Seeley & Co. Ltd, 1890)

Davidson, J., *Most Green Buildings – So Far – Aren't Even Close to Being Carbon-Neutral* (Curbed, 3 Feb., 2022)

Goodier, J.H., *Dictionary of Painting and Decorating*, second edition (London: C. Griffin, 1974)

'Historical Linseed Oil / Colophony Varnishes Formulations: Study of their molecular composition with micro-chemical chromatographic techniques', *Microchemical Journal*, 126 (2015) pp. 200–13 (Amsterdam: Elsevier)

Horie, C.V., *Materials for Conservation: Organic Consolidants, Adhesives and Coatings* (Oxford: Butterworths, 1987)

https://apt.memberclicks.net/assets/Publications/Bulletin/2021/52.4/52.4%20Gibbs%20and%20Wonson.pdf

https://healthybuilding.net/blog/600-low-voc-dont-stop-there

https://www.curbed.com/2022/02/green-building-claims-carbon-neutral-environment.html?utm_campaign=curbed.socialflow&utm_content=curbed&utm_medium=social&utm_source=twitter&fbclid=IwAR02pAhV6VUh4ElcSUUdQgeYRDDIRaymXd9HSXsHfvT1VRVdlvFucGeE9QE#comments

Hurst, A.E., *Painting and Decorating* (London: C. Griffin, 1949)

Hurst, G.H., *Painters' Colours, Oils and Varnishes: A Practical Manual* (London: 1892)

*Interior Wall Decoration: Practical Working Methods for Plain and Decorative Finishes, New and Standard Treatments* (London: reprint by Forgotten Books, 2018; original publ. Frederick J. Drake & Co., 1924)

*Mortise & Tenon Magazine* (Sedgwick, ME)

Norfolk Wood Tar Project Report, Michael Knights (Norfolk County Council) in partnership with University of East Anglia and Forestry Commission https://spab1877.sharepoint.com/sites/SPABCompany/Shared%20Documents/Forms/AllItems.aspx?id=%2Fsites%2FSPABCompany%2FShared%20Documents%2FOUTREACH%2FMembership%2FRegional%20Groups%2FRG%20Events%2FWood%20Tar%20Project%20Norfolk%201999%20BW%20print%20friendly%5Fcompressed%2Epdf&parent=%2Fsites%2FSPABCompany%2FShared%20Documents%2FOUTREACH%2FMembership%2FRegional%20Groups%2FRG%20Events&p=true

*NOT ZERO: How 'Net Zero' Targets Disguise Climate Inaction* https://www.corporateaccountability.org/wp-content/uploads/2020/10/NOT-ZERO-How-net-zero-targets-disguise-climate-inaction-FINAL.pdf

Parker, G., *Workin' in the Woods – Toil for Timber in Early New Brunswick* (Sackville, NB: 2015)

*Preservation Technology – Readings from the APT Bulletin* (Springfield, IL: The Association for Preservation Technology International, 2008)

Schulten, S., *A History of America in 100 Maps* (London: The British Library, 2018)

Snelling, J., *Painting and Decorating Defects Cause and Cure* (London: E. & F.N. Spon Ltd: 1966)

Suhr, M. and Hunt, R., *Old House Eco Handbook – A Practical Guide to Retrofitting for Energy Efficiency and Sustainability*, second edition (London: SPAB, 2019)

Vanderwalker, F.N., *The Mixing of Colors and Paints* (Chicago: Frederick J. Drake, 1924)

Van Groesen, M., Tise, L.E., *Theodore de Bry – America* (Köln, Taschen, 2019)

Wolf, N., *The Golden Age of Dutch and Flemish Painting* (Munich: Prestel, 2019)